The Love Stories of the Bible Speak

Also by Shannon Bream

Finding the Bright Side: The Art of Chasing What Matters

*The Women of the Bible Speak: The Wisdom of
16 Women and Their Lessons for Today*

*The Mothers and Daughters of the Bible Speak:
Lessons on Faith from Nine Biblical Families*

THE
LOVE
STORIES
OF THE
BIBLE SPEAK

13 BIBLICAL LESSONS ON ROMANCE, FRIENDSHIP, AND FAITH

SHANNON BREAM

FOX NEWS books

HarperCollins books may be purchased for educational, business, or sales promotional use. For information, please email the Special Markets Department at SPsales@harpercollins.com.

Fox News Books imprint and logo are trademarks of Fox News Network, LLC.

FIRST EDITION

Library of Congress Cataloging-in-Publication Data has been applied for.

ISBN 978-0-06-322605-0

23 24 25 26 27 LBC 5 4 3 2 1

My Beloved Sheldon

Of all the love stories God will ever script,
ours will always be my favorite

We love because He first loved us.

—1 John 4:19

CONTENTS

CONTENTS

I cry at weddings . . . a lot. It really doesn't matter how well I know the bride or groom; I'm just awestruck at the leap of faith two people are willing to take in vowing their lives and their hearts to each other. I remember being giddy with excitement as I walked to the altar, deeply in love with Sheldon and excited about the future we imagined we'd have together. Just before both my father and step-dad walked me down the aisle, my father looked at me and began to cry. His emotion confused me a bit because I was ready to joyfully sprint to the front of the church and get this show on the road!

Midway through the ceremony, the pastor had Sheldon and me turn to face our families and friends and I was shocked at what I saw. His three sisters were literally sobbing, to the point that I suddenly wondered if they didn't want their brother to marry me. And that confusion is what poor couples must feel when they see me crying through their ceremonies!

It's all a matter of perspective. Everyone at the wedding is thinking about that magical ingredient our hearts all long for: love. It's inspired captivating poems and sweeping symphonies, grand gestures and ultimate sacrifices. But it's also found in the more mundane decisions like letting someone else have the last piece of birthday cake or caring for their wounds—physical or emotional. You see, everyone at that marriage ceremony may be thinking of a different facet of love. The young bride, like I was, is often bursting with optimism and thoughts of romance (though we had certainly walked through some fires before we got to the church that day). Others may be remembering their own heartbreaks, knowing from experience that the road ahead will test every syllable of the vows the couple is about to utter—and that the community who stands around them will make all the difference. Some attendees will likely be taking their own trip down memory lane, remembering the day they said, "I do" and wondering how they so quickly fast-forwarded to the blessing of becoming grandparents—seemingly overnight.

The important point is that love is a lot bigger than just romantic feelings. Even at a wedding, where we gather to celebrate what many of us consider the most straightforward form of romance, we see how much bigger and more varied love is for everyone in the congregation. Similarly, in the Bible there are all kinds of "love" stories, from the romance of Song of Solomon to the friendship of Paul and Barnabas to the love of Christ for us.

Love is central to the Christian life, and particularly, the way God defines it, not the world. I was struck by all of these themes when I sat down to re-read 1 Corinthians 13 not long ago. If you've been to many church weddings, you've likely heard it—repeatedly! It's the most popular scripture reading of all time for marriage ceremonies. Someone even gave us a beautiful framed version, done in calligraphy, as a wedding gift. It's an inspiring, challenging reminder of what true love is actually supposed to be and how we should see it play out in our own lives.

The first four verses begin by telling us that without love, pretty much anything else we do is worthless, void, meaningless. Forget power, money, fame—all the things the world values—in the economy of heaven, love is the only currency that matters. That's the first lesson: Love is not optional.

If I speak in the tongues of men and angels, but have not love, I am only a resounding gong or a clanging cymbal. If I have the gift of prophecy and can fathom all mysteries and all knowledge, and if I have faith that can move mountains, but have not love, I am nothing. If I give all I possess to the poor and surrender my body to the flames, but have not love, I gain nothing.
1 Corinthians 13:1-4

To recap: you can have the best oratorical skills, actually be able to see the future and understand the deepest puzzles of the universe, have unwavering faith, give away everything you have to those in need and sacrifice your own life—but without love, all of that is completely pointless.

Those verses should get our attention. We can do and be and strive, even doing things that are wholly positive, but if we are operating from anything less than the purest motivations of love—we might as well have stayed home on the couch eating bonbons. It's *so* important that we learn to love that Paul writes,

The entire law is summed up in a single command: "Love your neighbor as yourself." Galatians 5:14

In that same passage, Paul admonishes us to "serve one another in love." (Galatians 5:13b) So, we know love should be the underpinning of all that we do in this life, and that the definition of that word itself sets an incredibly high standard.

But that brings us to the second lesson. What is love? It's not what the world tells us, or whatever our emotions tell us it is. We can only truly understand and share love in its purest form if we allow God to show us the way. As you'll see in the pages ahead, all true love is rooted in God. He is not only the source of love He *is* love. He created Adam and Eve in His own image, to be in eternal fellowship with Him. He poured—and is still pouring—out His heart into the very breath in our lungs.

I often pray the Lord will allow me to see my true reasons for taking particular actions, and I cringe at times when He holds up a mirror. Did I run that errand for someone simply to help them in a time of need, or do I want them to like me more and think I'm a nice person? Am I motivated out of love for them . . . or for my own self-image? If I'm being honest with myself, sometimes the good deed is more selfish than it would appear from the outside.

There's also this conundrum: finding the balance in "speaking out of love." You know the drill. You see someone struggling, but you just know if they'd get their lives together and quit self-sabotaging themselves their journey would be much smoother. I mean, look at how well your own life is going! You decide it's time to confront them—you know, for their own good. Please hit the pause button for just a second. Search your heart. Am I ignoring the plank in my own eye in order to tend to their splinter? Am I approaching them with some secret air of superiority, deigning to reach down and pull them up from the mud without looking at the splatters on my own shoes? No doubt, real love will act to approach and assist others, but let's remember how Christ did this. More to come on that!

Here's where it gets tricky.

Love is patient, love is kind. It does not envy, it does not boast, it is not proud. It is not rude, it is not self-seeking, it is not easily angered, it keeps no record of wrongs. Love

does not delight in evil but rejoices with the truth. It always protects, always trusts, always hopes, always perseveres. Love never fails.

1 Corinthians 13:4–8a

I'm not gonna lie, plenty of conviction is hitting me right between the eyes as I read through that list. I've fallen short of all those measures on multiple occasions. By the way, are we supposed to love our fellow motorists? Because that "patient" and "not easily angered" stuff can be tough to live out.

But now for the good news!

God's love for every person reading this page or hearing these words is perfect and unstoppable. It is unbounded, unblemished, and unconditional. It doesn't matter where we've been or what we've done, His love for us doesn't dim. You don't have to do a single thing to earn it, and no one can take it away.

For I am convinced that neither death nor life, nor angels nor demons, neither the present nor the future, nor any powers, neither height nor depth, nor anything else in all creation, will be able to separate us from the love of God that is in Christ Jesus our LORD.

Romans 8:38–39

What could be more comforting and hopeful than that? The God of the universe sees you, knows you, and adores you without hesitation.

As we grow in Him, and allow His goodness to infuse our souls and our lives, we increase in our ability to love others in the same way. We'll never fully arrive at perfection this side of heaven, but if we're willing to follow His example, He'll give us what we need in order to make peace with that highly-irritating family member, backstabbing co-worker, or the neighbor who decided to buy a rooster. Sometimes I have to pray that God will give me the *willingness* to try to walk that path, then we can talk about making actual progress.

His love covers and surrounds us, it compels us to be better and is there to heal us when we get it wrong. Everything He models for us, He also equips us to live out.

The Bible is full of stories of people failing to live up to God's standard. We see ungodly interpretations of love in the toxic relationships of the Bible, from the foolishness of Samson to the arrogance of Xerxes to the cowardice of Adam and Eve. But we also see God's mercy for His misguided children.

On the other hand, in the Song of Solomon, we see the joy and desire of two people who can't wait to get married. It reminds us that God created us with all of those yearnings for passion and connection. We have the privilege of witnessing Ruth's selfless love for her mother-in-law, Naomi, when she could have easily walked away from a desperate situation. Jonathan was so devoted to his friend David that he pledged his loyalty to him, rather than to his murderous father, King Saul. And all throughout the New Testament we witness the many friendships of Paul on his missionary journeys, relationships that served as the foundation of the early church.

In some ways these stories confirm our cultural assumptions about love, and in other ways, they challenge them. Through studying them, we can begin to truly understand how to love in the way God does.

Each of us is on our own journey too, of both realizing how

deeply God loves us and of learning how to love others the way He does. In the pages to come we'll read about all kinds of love stories: romance, friendship, community, and more. Some are pure, as God designed. Some are a devastating mess. If you've read any of my previous books, you already know I think the Lord can work through both scenarios. I look forward to taking this adventure right along with you.

ROMANTIC LOVE

SONG OF SOLOMON

The Gift of Love

Song of Solomon

It's the best-known love story in the Bible, but I'm not going to lie: I've often been intimidated by the Song of Solomon (also called the Song of Songs). It's a beautiful book full of flowery language, intimate moments, and gushy sentiments. It was too racy to end up in our Sunday School lessons, leaving us giggling as young kids flipping through the pages and trying to understand what the fuss was all about. Recently, I was visiting a church with friends and saw the sermon was going to be about this mysterious book. My first thought as I looked around at the mostly twentysomething congregation: awkward! I haven't heard many pastors tackle the Song of Solomon from the pulpit, and I was intrigued by the deep, practical lessons he so eloquently outlined for us.

The principles woven throughout this romantic book stand in such stark contrast to much of what modern society tells us about relationships. They show us the truth about God's design for romance, love, and sex. He created it all! In Song of Solomon, we're given an insider's view into a couple longing to be together but committed to the virtue of waiting to awaken love at its proper time. They shower each other with praise, respect, and admiration—along with their obvious physical attraction. Again and again we see their desire to finally join together in marriage, while respecting the boundaries keeping them apart.

When you've found the one you love, the wait can be agonizing. I remember my wedding day, waiting in the children's area of the church. My bridesmaids and I gathered around on tiny chairs and tables, finishing our make-up and watching the clock tick slowly down to the moment I would finally meet Sheldon at the altar. I was able to peek out the windows and see family and friends as they walked across the parking lot and into the church entrance. Excitement and impatience bubbled through my chest. I wasn't scared to walk down the aisle. I was like a fired-up racehorse trapped in the starting gate. *Let's get this show on the road, people!* Like the bride in the Song of Solomon I trusted that I had found a man of great integrity, and I was crazy about him.

There has been plenty of debate over the centuries, and it still continues, about whether Song of Solomon is a broader allegory about God's love for Israel or Christ's for the church. I think it's always possible that the words of Scripture are pointing us to the bigger picture of God's unconditional love and plan of redemption for humanity, but many scholars do believe Song of Solomon is a literal love story—one that's full of practical instruction on how we should cherish our relationships and our spouses. And while it doesn't mention God by name, His wisdom is ever-present in the story. Like the book of Esther, which also has no direct mention of God, Song of Solomon still contains His truths.

In Esther, we witness God's saving care for His people through the persons of Esther and Mordecai. Here we see the gift of marriage specifically crafted by God's plans.

This book is full of intense and heartfelt poetry, and it contains some of the deepest expressions of love and devotion ever written in the ancient world. The dialogue between Solomon, the "Beloved," and his bride pulses with their love and desire for each other. It also shows us the beauty and power of our natural yearnings. Much like fire, which can be destructive without boundaries, passion alone can be disastrous. But just like a flame contained and channeled into a resource for preparing delicious meals, creating cozy warmth, or refining valuable metals, passion can be incredibly beneficial—the cement for a lifelong commitment. And that is the context of Song of Solomon, a celebration of courtship and marriage.

The name alone tells us how significant this book is. Solomon was known for his wisdom and is credited with writing more than 1,000 songs. But this one was deemed the greatest of them all, a love song to beat all others. King Solomon himself is widely believed to be both the author and the bridegroom in this ballad. He and his bride, a Shulamite woman, are enamored with each other. The language is so colorful, that some ancient scholars thought it best for anyone who may struggle with lust to avoid studying it. Early Christian writer Origen in his book, *Commentary on the Song of Songs,* cautioned:

> I advise and counsel everyone who is not yet rid of the vexations of flesh and blood and has not ceased to feel the passion of his bodily nature, to refrain completely from

reading this little book and the things that will be said about it.[1]

That didn't discourage theologians over the years, those who knew how helpful the lovely words of this book could be for anyone looking to God's direction in the area of romance—so let's dive in!

The Bride

From the very beginning, we see that the bride is clear about her desire for Solomon.

> Let him kiss me with the kisses of his mouth—
> for your love is more delightful than wine.
> Pleasing is the fragrance of your perfumes;
> your name is like perfume poured out.
> No wonder the young women love you!
>   Song of Solomon 1:2–3

This is no shrinking violet afraid to tell her Beloved exactly how she feels. Her senses are overwhelmed with everything about this man. The bride also praises his name, meaning his reputation and character are pleasing to those who are observing him. She sees why so many others would love to be his potential bride, and she has no shame in the words of adoration she's sharing.

She goes on to describe her own appearance, just as she will celebrate her bridegroom's.

Dark am I, yet lovely,
daughters of Jerusalem,
dark like the tents of Kedar,
like the tent curtains of Solomon.
Do not stare at me because I am dark,
because I am darkened by the sun.
My mother's sons were angry with me
and made me take care of the vineyards;
my own vineyard I had to neglect.
  Songs 1:5–6

It's important to keep in mind that for the bride and her cultural context, her reference to dark skin meant primarily that she had not had the luxury of staying indoors. She had worked outside, instead of living a more privileged life. Her "angry" brothers had assigned her to work out in the fields, the verse suggesting that she'd had to ignore her own care in the process.

This bride also openly declares that she wants to be with her groom.

Tell me, you whom I love,
where you graze your flock
and where you rest your sheep at midday.
Why should I be like a veiled woman
beside the flocks of your friends?
  Song of Solomon 1:7

She wants to know where he is, so she can find him. The reference to a "veiled woman" was likely an allusion to a woman of questionable morals. This bride didn't want to be mistaken in that way; she wanted to proudly show her face in the presence of her man. Their heartfelt compliments trade back and forth in this first chapter, making their intentions unmistakable. We'll look at Solomon's perspective a bit later.

In chapter 2, the bride calls herself "a rose of Sharon, a lily of the valleys" (v. 1). It's not a boastful statement, but probably an acknowledgment of how he has made her view herself. These flowers were lovely, but also abundant. She is not setting herself above every other woman. Solomon sees her as pure and lovely, and he responds:

> **Like a lily among thorns**
> **is my darling among the young women.**
>   Songs 2:2

In his eyes, she is exceptional. The love that she has received and given has made her own beauty bloom: the daughters of Jerusalem call her "most beautiful of women." (Songs 1:8, 5:9)

The groom's words of praise have made her feel confident and attractive. Think about the power of words between spouses. It is so easy in the heat of an argument, or in the middle of a string of frustrations, to lash out with words that deeply wound and scar. We will all have times of conflict in our marriages, but how we choose to engage will either strengthen or chip away at the foundation of our relationship. It can require enormous restraint not to criticize and blame when tensions are high. Sheldon and I have disagreed just like any other couple, but from the beginning we made the concrete decision not to cross the line into weaponizing the way we talk to each other. If that means walking out the door or screaming into a bedazzled throw pillow, so be it! I've been so mad that my insides felt like a nuclear bomb had gone off, but I don't ever want to live with the regret of tearing apart our sacred bond with venomous words.

Instead, over the years, Sheldon has made me believe in myself with his steady encouragement and cheerleading. It's not that we never get it wrong, but we've purposed that we will mostly get it right. I don't want anyone else vying for the role of being my husband's number one fan. Nope. That's my title and I'm willing to fight for it. I want my words to encourage and challenge him, to let him know that I'm impressed by his integrity and thankful for his character. I also think he's incredibly handsome, and what husband doesn't want to hear that?! Solomon and his bride show us the beauty of lavishing each other with positive reinforcement.

The bride continues to praise her groom:

Like an apple tree among the trees of the forest
is my beloved among the young men.
I delight to sit in his shade,
and his fruit is sweet to my taste.
> **Songs 2:3**

This is starting to make me think my attempts at love notes are so amateur! It's interesting to note that it would be unusual to find an apple tree in your average forest. Is this bride signaling that Solomon is a rare standout among other men? And remember how she lamented working in the blazing sun? She's now praising her groom as a place of shade, suggesting she finds security and comfort with him.

In this chapter we also see phrases that will be repeated again in the book. In verse seven, the bride urges:

Daughters of Jerusalem, I charge you
by the gazelles and by the does of the field:
Do not arouse or awaken love
until it so desires.
    Songs 2:7

Take note of that admonition not to stir up love just yet. This couple was not yet joined in marriage, but they were definitely looking forward to it.

Also threaded through her words of admiration for him and her growing excitement about finding their way to each other is another phrase we'll see again: "My beloved is mine and I am his." (Songs 2:16) She is secure in what she's found with her groom. Solomon's love has given the bride confidence in their relationship. This expression of mutual love and assurance is so powerful that in the Jewish tradition, this Hebrew phrase—*ani l'dodi v' dodi li*—is inscribed on wedding bands and marriage certificates as the ultimate statement of commitment.

We next find the bride in the middle of the night, in what appears to be a dream.

All night long on my bed
I looked for the one my heart loves;
I looked for him but did not find him.
I will get up now and go about the city,
through its streets and squares;
I will search for the one my heart loves.
So I looked for him but did not find him.
The watchmen found me

as they made their rounds in the city.
"Have you seen the one my heart loves?"
    Songs 3:1–4

In this dream, the bride's heart was emboldened to roam the city looking for the man she adored. She sounds downright miserable to be separated from him, and what joy when she found him.

Scarcely had I passed them
when I found the one my heart loves.
I held him and would not let him go
till I had brought him to my mother's house,
to the room of the one who conceived me.
    Songs 3:4

She's dreaming not only of finding her Beloved, but also of something much more lasting—taking him to her family. She wants this relationship, but with the approval of her mother. In the ancient Near East, the mother was often the one who arranged the wedding ceremony and celebrations. This is not the call for a fleeting affair; it's a picture of wanting this love to follow the boundaries and traditions of purity and permanence.

The bride closes out chapter 3 by describing a glorious wedding processional.

Who is this coming up from the wilderness
like a column of smoke,
perfumed with myrrh and incense

made from all the spices of the merchant?
Look! It is Solomon's carriage,
escorted by sixty warriors,
the noblest of Israel,
all of them wearing the sword,
all experienced in battle,
each with his sword at his side,
prepared for the terrors of the night.
King Solomon made for himself the carriage;
he made it of wood from Lebanon.
Its posts he made of silver,
its base of gold.
Its seat was upholstered with purple,
its interior inlaid with love.

    Songs 3:6–10a

My first thought when reading this was that it portrays the arrival of the groom. But some noted theologians say it could actually represent the bride arriving in a carriage and procession that Solomon himself had arranged for her. In the question, "Who is this?" the Hebrew translation of "this" refers to a singular female. That would suggest that her bridegroom had made sure she would have the glories of a majestic entrance, riding in a spectacular carriage and surrounded by noble warriors committed to her protection.

The bride then urged the women of Jerusalem to come see the groom.

Daughters of Jerusalem, come out,
and look, you daughters of Zion.

Look on King Solomon wearing a crown,
the crown with which his mother crowned him
on the day of his wedding,
the day his heart rejoiced.
    Songs 3:10b-11

If you've read *Mothers and Daughters of the Bible Speak,* you know all about King Solomon's mother, Bathsheba. She fought to make sure he assumed the throne, and it is fitting that she would be there to share in his joyous wedding day.

In chapter 5, we once again see the bride dreaming of—and yearning for—her groom. She tells the Daughters of Jerusalem that if they could locate him, "Tell him I am faint with love." (Songs 5:8) In response they ask what makes him so special, and we now get to see the bride's grand portrayal of the groom she desperately longs for.

My beloved is radiant and ruddy,
outstanding among ten thousand.
His head is purest gold;
his hair is wavy
and black as a raven.
His eyes are like doves
by the water streams,
washed in milk,
mounted like jewels.
His cheeks are like beds of spice
yielding perfume.
His lips are like lilies
dripping with myrrh.

His arms are rods of gold
set with topaz.
His body is like polished ivory
decorated with lapis lazuli.
His legs are pillars of marble
set on bases of pure gold.
His appearance is like Lebanon,
choice as its cedars.
His mouth is sweetness itself;
he is altogether lovely.
This is my beloved, this is my friend,
daughters of Jerusalem.
    Songs 5:10–16

Now that's a description!

I can't imagine many of us sit around describing our spouse by talking about their lips as lilies or their arms as rods of gold. Those initial sparks of physical attraction can cement the early years of a relationship, but how many long-married couples wax poetic about each other's body parts over the breakfast table? We don't do those things, because "real life" gets in the way, and because our connection with our spouse grows and evolves into something much deeper than mere physical passion.

But the lovers in the Song of Songs challenge us to think about that some more. To sit and look at our spouse—really look at them—and to notice all the little things that maybe we stopped paying attention to, is an act of deep love and selflessness. It's an act that says, "I cherish this person from head to toe." It's not that physical desire and mutual respect should compete with each other within our marriages. They should always serve as a complement, and by feeding one you often nourish the other.

I'm reminded of the bestselling book *The Five Love Languages* by Gary Chapman. Like many young couples we were given a copy by our pastor as a part of our pre-marital counseling. Early on in our relationship, I had wrongly assumed that everyone was motivated and encouraged by the same things. While Sheldon and I were dating, I put together an elaborate treasure hunt with clues, gifts, and cards all over Tallahassee for his birthday. It was the first of his that we had celebrated as a couple. I went all out, roping in family members and spending days planning the whole thing. When we ended the night in a candlelit gazebo overlooking a little lake, I expected him to gush over the details and presents. There was none of that, and I was very disappointed. Why wasn't this guy doing a cartwheel?! Turns out my husband is motivated by acts of service. I would have been better off washing his car.

For me, it's definitely words of affirmation, and I think there's a strong argument that Solomon and his bride were into that too. Again and again we see them lavish praise and adoration on each other. We also witness them complimenting each other in front of other people. I've found in twenty-seven years of marriage that there are few things I appreciate more than my husband bragging about me—in front of me. It's reassuring and romantic to know he's happy to let others know he made a good choice. Solomon and his bride left no doubt.

Their story also clearly telegraphs to people of faith that God doesn't want us to ignore this facet of our humanity. The poetic language, beautiful and direct, teaches us to approach sexuality with wonder and care instead of vulgarity or fear. By engaging our emotions with this love song, the book gives us an imaginative vision of an ideal relationship that's more powerful than simple factual description.

What about Solomon? What was his view of this bride thrilled at the thought of finally becoming his wife? He too saw his adored as the pinnacle of physical perfection, a young woman with no flaws at all. We first see him speak of her in chapter 1:

> I liken you, my darling, to a mare
> among Pharaoh's chariot horses.
> Your cheeks are beautiful with earrings,
> your neck with strings of jewels.
> We will make you earrings of gold,
> studded with silver. . . .
> How beautiful you are, my darling!
> Oh, how beautiful!
> Your eyes are doves.
>   Songs 1:9–11, 15

He was besotted, freely showering her with descriptive appreciation. Solomon again compliments her in chapter 2:

> My dove in the clefts of the rock,
> in the hiding places on the mountainside,
> show me your face,

let me hear your voice;
for your voice is sweet,
and your face is lovely.
> Songs 2:14

This language echoes what we heard from the bride earlier, and will see throughout Song of Solomon. The couple appears to be separated, longing to be together, and searching for each other.

In the very next verse, there is concern about what could interrupt their joy.

Catch for us the foxes,
the little foxes
that ruin the vineyards,
our vineyards that are in bloom.
> Songs 2:15

Scholars and various interpretations of Scripture differ on who the speaker is here. In any case, the principle is a good one: take note of the things that could ruin a relationship. What are the little foxes that could ruin the fruit of our marital vineyards?

The world will constantly throw temptations our way, whether it's something that seems as common as complaining about our spouse—or the invitation to break our marriage vows with someone else. Every day resentments can chip away at our respect and admiration for each other. Avoiding tough conversations, getting lost in online shopping or porn—there are plenty of little foxes out there looking to sow discord. Rarely does someone float down the aisle to their beloved and wake up the next day deciding they hate everything about them. There are small hurts and slights and selfish behavior that begin to chip away at the promises we make to each other at the altar. When we rationalize a work relationship that's gotten too chummy or constantly grumble about our spouse to someone else, we are inviting the little foxes in. When we decide to hide our secret purchases or undermine our spouse to our children, we open the door to real damage. It is always the right time to catch the little foxes and toss them out of our sacred vineyards.

The groom spends almost the entirety of chapter 4 wooing and complimenting his bride again. Some of the imagery may seem silly translated into modern-day English, but the descriptions all have deep meaning—Solomon's best attempt to tell his bride just how enamored he was with her.

> How beautiful you are, my darling!
> Oh, how beautiful!
> Your eyes behind your veil are doves.
> Your hair is like a flock of goats
> descending from the hills of Gilead.
> Your teeth are like a flock of sheep just shorn,
> coming up from the washing.
> Each has its twin;
> not one of them is alone.
> Your lips are like a scarlet ribbon;
> your mouth is lovely.
> Songs 4:1–3

He continues on for several verses more, including this passage:

You have stolen my heart, my sister, my bride;
you have stolen my heart
with one glance of your eyes,
with one jewel of your necklace.
How delightful is your love, my sister, my bride!
How much more pleasing is your love than wine,
and the fragrance of your perfume
more than any spice!
Your lips drop sweetness as the honeycomb, my bride;
milk and honey are under your tongue.
The fragrance of your garments
is like the fragrance of Lebanon.
You are a garden locked up, my sister, my bride;
you are a spring enclosed, a sealed fountain.
    Songs 4:9–12

If the word "sister" catches your eye, keep in mind that in the customs and language of the day the words "sister" and "brother" were regularly used as terms of endearment between husbands and wives. Some say it would be like using the word "sweetheart" as we do today. I think we could also imagine that it was a pronouncement that they shared the same faith in the God of Israel, their heavenly Father.

In chapter 6, Solomon told his bride she was so beautiful he couldn't even make eye contact with her!

Turn your eyes from me;
they overwhelm me.
    Songs 6:5

He also called her "unique" and noted, "The young women saw her and called her blessed . . ." (Songs 6:9) One of the most instructive and beautiful things about this relationship is that others outside of it were able to see how special these two were. Have you ever dated a guy that all your friends hated, and you spent a lot of emotion and time trying to convince them they didn't see the "real him"? That's not happening in this relationship. Earlier, we saw how the bride bragged on him and talked about how all the young women would be happy to be at his side. Here, in chapter 6, Solomon is doing the same. He's noting that other people see her great value and beauty.

And here's where the romance really heats up. Chapter 7 consists of these two lovebirds expressing their desire to be together. He ticks through every part of her body, admiring and yearning for it. She doesn't hold back either, returning his eagerness to be united. If you're fanning yourself while reading this amorous back-and-forth, remember that God created all of this. He could have simply made us machines for reproduction. But unlike nearly every other being to ever exist, God set humans apart to have real pleasure in our physical relationships—within the boundaries he created. Again, not because he wants to make our lives boring—quite the opposite. His gift to us is the beauty and intimacy of truly connecting with someone we've pledged our life to and who has given us the same in return. It's in the midst of that security and commitment that we can fully enjoy everything God intended for us. And if we've gotten that wrong at any point, God is a forgiving Father ready to help us work toward His ideal for how we relate to one another.

In the final chapter of this all-time great love song, we see the bride extol the virtues of love itself.

Place me like a seal over your heart,
like a seal on your arm;
for love is as strong as death,
its jealousy unyielding as the grave.
It burns like blazing fire,
like a mighty flame.
Many waters cannot quench love;
rivers cannot sweep it away.
If one were to give
all the wealth of one's house for love,
it would be utterly scorned.
   Songs 8: 6–7

There's a lot of truth and passion packed into just two verses.

She asked her groom to place her as a seal over his heart and on his arm. That speaks to the permanence of this relationship. She declared that love is as strong as death. Who can run from death? No one. Love can be that overwhelming and all-encompassing. And the picture of a flame reminds us that it can be both beautiful and destructive, depending on how it's handled. You can't drown love, and you can't sweep it away. If you tried to stack up every material thing you owned against love, it would be pointless. Its value is beyond worldly measure!

This bride and groom remind us just how powerful and precious love and the hope for a lifetime bond can be. We should cherish the gift of romance and marriage, nurture and feed it. As our relationships mature, we shouldn't put them on autopilot. Maybe we aren't as gifted as the writer of the Song of Solomon, but it doesn't take long to tuck a quick note into your spouse's lunchbox or onto their dashboard. What about fighting for unity instead of fighting to always be right? Love requires sacrifice. We have to handle it as a delicate treasure, with care and attention. It calls us to put someone else first, to want the very best for them, and to grow beyond our selfishness. As my husband often says, "When you're busy trying to put the other person first, you both wind up happy."

Prayer: Father, thank you for the divine gifts of love, romance, and marriage. Help us to remember that You created all of these treasures specifically for us. Guide us so that we treat them with respect and find great joy in them! Where we have strayed from Your perfect plan, repair our hearts and move us forward in forgiveness. Show us how to love our spouses with abandon.

SAMSON AND DELILAH

Mercy and Restoration

Judges 13–16

Let's face it, in the Bible, as in modern times, sometimes romances are rocky and ultimately destructive. We can't look at the love stories in Scripture without digging into this massively dysfunctional hookup. If you heard the tale of Samson and Delilah growing up, told in Judges 13–16, you may visualize him as a Fabio type—rippling with muscles and a glorious, flowing mane. It turns out that isn't exactly accurate, but as a kid in Sunday School I certainly pictured Samson as a guy who would be on the front of one of those racy romance novels on display at the library. The story of Samson and Delilah has inspired works of art, operas, and movies. It's easily one of the most well-known stories of the Old Testament, yet this couple is a case study into how to get nearly everything about romance wrong. But as with every ancient biblical story of woe, this one is chock-full of lessons for us today. And while we will eventually focus on the deeply flawed relationship of Samson and Delilah, there's plenty to learn about Samson before we get there.

Samson

There are no accidents in Scripture, so it feels deeply important that the messy saga of this troubled couple takes place alongside the story of one of the most stable, healthy marriages we get to see in Scripture: Samson's parents. He actually grew up in a home with a mother and father who were committed to both God and to each other. It all started with a heavenly visit to Samson's mother, identified only as Manoah's wife.

> The angel of the LORD appeared to her and said, "You are barren and childless, but you are going to become pregnant and give birth to a son."
> **Judges 13:3**

Many theologians have held that this Angel was Christ Himself, visiting Earth before He later came in human form. It's interesting that the story of one of the Bible's strongest, most privileged characters begins with a childless woman, who would have suffered shame in her culture for her infertility. Childlessness was one of the greatest burdens a woman in ancient Israel could bear. Without a child, her husband's name would be erased, and she would have no part in carrying forward the blessing of God to the next generation. Like Sarah, Hannah, and Elizabeth, Manoah's wife struggled with infertility, and like them she may have felt abandoned by God.

In each of those stories we have beautiful reminders that God is aware of the heartache of infertility. Often the delays and trials of that struggle are part of a grander plan He is weaving, in His timing. There are times when God's answers aren't the ones we pray for and suffer anguish over, but He is uniquely mindful of everything that our hearts desire. Psalm 34:18 reminds us:

The LORD is close to the brokenhearted
and saves those who are crushed in spirit.

If you are walking through a season of waiting on a child you fear may never come, you are not alone.

We have no background about whether Samson's mother may have petitioned God over her lack of a child, but she wound up on a very exclusive list. There are only two women in the Bible who got a personal visit from an angel to tell them about their pregnancies in advance, and in the unlikeliest of situations: Manoah's wife and Mary herself. That's some pretty privileged company! And just as the angel Gabriel had details for Mary, the Angel of the Lord gave Samson's mother some very specific instructions:

Now see to it that you drink no wine or other fermented drink and that you do not eat anything unclean. You will become pregnant and have a son whose head is never to be touched by a razor because the boy is to be a Nazirite, dedicated to God from the womb. He will take the lead in delivering Israel from the hands of the Philistines.
Judges 13:4–5

This was a lot to digest: a visit from the Angel of the Lord, news that her barren womb would soon hold a son, the boy must follow sacred vows, and would help Israel to escape its brutal oppressors. It's notable that Samson appears to be the only "lifelong" Nazirite we meet in Scripture. Generally, the vow was taken for a short period of time. A Nazirite vow didn't just mean no haircuts. God also required Nazirites to not consume wine or strong drink—or even grape juice or grapes! A Nazirite also could never touch a dead body (Numbers 6:1-21). Samson's mother didn't question any of what she was told, and she went straight to her husband to share the news.

> **Then the woman went to her husband and told him, "A man of God came to me. He looked like an angel of God, very awesome. I didn't ask him where he came from, and he didn't tell me his name."**
> **Judges 13:6**

I love that Manoah didn't doubt her at all, or God. Instead, he only wanted even more information in order to be sure they got this right as parents who would work together on a glorious assignment. It's somewhat remarkable, since in other instances of prophesied children, the first response from one or both parents was often disbelief.

With miracle babies prophesied for once-barren mothers, it's understandable why they would have that reaction! But couples in the Bible who found themselves in this position were often split in their response. Sarah scoffed at the Lord's message though Abraham believed. Elizabeth rejoiced at Gabriel's news even as her husband Zechariah's doubt meant God rendered him mute until baby John arrived.

But Samson's parents were united from the very moment they learned their son, who would be no ordinary man, was on the way. Manoah prayed to God that He would "let the man of God you sent to *us* come again to teach *us* how to bring up the boy who is to be born." (Judges 13:8) In everything that Manoah said he referred to himself and his wife as a parenting team. God heard Manoah's prayer, and sent the Angel again—but once again, to his wife. This time, before the Angel was even allowed to speak, she ran to find her husband so he too could share in their conversation:

> The woman hurried to tell her husband, "He's here! The man who appeared to me the other day!"
> Judges 13:10

In her humility and in loyalty to her husband, Samson's mother automatically included Manoah in the revelation. Manoah pressed to hear again exactly how their coming son should be raised. The Angel repeated the instructions he'd given on His first visit, and Manoah—once again singling their partnership in marriage—said, "*We* would like you to stay until *we* prepare a young goat for you." (Judges 13:15) We see Manoah use the same language as the Angel prepared to leave, "What is your name, so that *we* may honor you when your word comes true?" (Judges 13:17)

The Angel told Manoah His name was "beyond understanding," (Judges 13:18) and then made one of the most epic departures of all time. He miraculously ascended up through the flame of their burnt offering (Judges 13:20). I think we'd probably all be as awestruck as Manoah:

> "We are doomed to die!" he said to his wife. "We have seen God!"
> But his wife answered, "If the LORD had meant to kill us, he would not have accepted a burnt offering and grain

offering from our hands, nor shown us all these things or now told us this."

Judges 13:22–23

Notice how she responded to his grave concerns, not with laughter or condescension. Instead she offered calm, comfort, and common sense. This was a couple in a healthy marriage.

I've got to admit the roles in this story would likely be reversed in my house. I am an "I-need-to-know-the-absolute-worst-case-scenario-and-plan-accordingly" kind of wife. I extrapolate innocuous, stray comments as evidence of trouble brewing up ahead! *What exactly did it mean when she said the Lord prompted her to pray for me?!* Fortunately, God has blessed me with a "you-need-to-calm-down-none-of-that-is-probably-ever-going-to-happen" kind of husband. I fully expect if an angel ever shows up at our house he's going to know he needs to start with Sheldon.

What these verses in Judges 13 show is that Samson was going to be born into a home where there was trust and respect between his parents. Manoah and his wife were devoted to God's will and to each other. What a contrast that would prove to be to the relationships Samson would chase in adulthood. Was his heart searching for what was so beautifully modeled for him at home, while his eyes were distracted by what seemed pleasing to him in the moment?

As Samson grew, his parents raised him according to the conditions of his Nazirite vow. But we eventually see that Samson's heart wasn't truly obedient to God's command, even if he maintained some outward appearance of dedication to holiness. Here's what should encourage every one of us: God was still able to use this sinful man for His purposes. Indeed, he was a judge over the

Israelites for twenty years and brutally punished their oppressors, the Philistines. But how much more could God have accomplished through a man who was fully obedient, humble, and honorable?

There were clues all along the way that Samson was capable of getting off track, so we shouldn't be shocked at what eventually transpired. Let's start with his first marriage, and you aren't alone if you don't remember hearing about that one! Here's how Judges 14 begins:

> Samson went down to Timnah and saw there a young Philistine woman. When he returned, he said to his father and mother, "I have seen a Philistine woman in Timnah; now get her for me as my wife."
> Judges 14:1–2

Well, that's rather blunt. And guess what? It was actually forbidden by the Law (Exodus 34:16, Deuteronomy 7:3), and Samson's parents weren't on board.

> His father and mother replied, "Isn't there an acceptable woman among your relatives or among all our people? Must you go to the uncircumcised Philistines to get a wife?"
> But Samson said to his father, "Get her for me. She's the right one for me."
> Judges 14:3

Samson was blinded by lust and selfishness. How could he know this woman was his soulmate when they hadn't even had a conversation?

Samson's parents must have struggled with the idea that a young man of Israel—much less one consecrated to God's service like their son—wanted to marry someone from outside the community, who presumably did not worship the God of Israel. We see again how Samson's parents were united in their opposition to his plan. While you might expect, in an ancient context, that only Samson's father would be mentioned, the Bible tells us that he spoke about this "to his father and mother," and "his father and mother replied" to him about his plans. It was a small but powerful witness to marital togetherness. "Togetherness" was the opposite of what Samson would find with his Philistine wife, and his rebellion against his parents' wise counsel was a mirror of Israel's continued defiance of God's commands.

As the family traveled down to see about this Philistine woman, something strange happened.

> As they approached the vineyards of Timnah, suddenly a young lion came roaring toward him. The Spirit of the LORD came powerfully upon him so that he tore the lion apart with his bare hands as he might have torn a young goat. But he told neither his father nor his mother what he had done.
> Judges 14:5b-6

And that's not all, when Samson traveled the same road on the return to go marry his first wife, he saw that the lion's carcass contained bees and honey.

> He scooped out the honey with his hands and ate as he went along. When he rejoined his parents, he gave them

some, and they too ate it. But he did not tell them that he
had taken the honey from the lion's carcass.
  Judges 14:9

This Nazirite young man, with no apparent second thought,
scooped honey out of the dead lion to eat on his journey. It's important to realize lions were not kosher animals (Leviticus 11:27)
and any food that had touched something unclean was also considered unclean (Leviticus 5:2-3). Samson was breaking the Le-
vitical law twice over by touching something unclean and eating
food that had touched something unclean.

And he involved others in his sin by giving that honey to his
unsuspecting parents! He also likely violated one of the pillars
of his personal oath. Remember the three requirements of the
Nazirite vow? No contact with a dead body, no wine or strong
drink (the oath is even more strict—no touching grapes!), and no
cutting his hair. He had probably broken the first rule of his vow,
though some scholars debate whether dead animals served to vi-
olate the command. Notably, this all happened in a vineyard off
the road, so if he wasn't touching grapes or drinking wine, he was
already skating on pretty thin ice.

All of this background opens our eyes to the fact that the
events involving the lion probably weren't random at all. Even
as Samson was courting a woman outside the people of God, he
was also compromising himself in other ways. He didn't love this
woman because he saw her heart for God (as Jewish Boaz saw in
the Moabitess, Ruth), but rather because he liked the looks of her.
Just as the people of Israel repeatedly rejected their heavenly Father's advice, Samson ignored the wisdom of his parents in order
to pursue his own desires.

How laughable to think we know better than our Heavenly Father. How often do we chase after something questionable because we "know" it's the right thing for us, even if it goes against what God has clearly instructed us to do? It's the most cringeworthy thing for me to look back over my life to see how easily I wandered at times, straying down a rocky path I thought I could manage. I don't know about you, but I've been capable of some world-class rationalizations over the years. What could be more foolish than thinking a choice I make in conflict with the God of the Universe is going to end well? Trust me—it won't—and it certainly didn't for Samson.

Samson's short-lived marriage to the Philistine woman ended in terrible tragedy. At his wedding feast (the Hebrew word here is literally "drinking feast"—tough place to be committed to a Nazirite vow), he gave a challenge to his Philistine guests, and it came with a hefty wager.

> "Let me tell you a riddle," Samson said to them. "If you can give me the answer within the seven days of the feast, I will give you thirty linen garments and thirty sets of clothes. If you can't tell me the answer, you must give me thirty linen garments and thirty sets of clothes."
> Judges 14:12–13

The Philistines accepted the terms and asked for the riddle.

> "Out of the eater, something to eat;
> out of the strong, something sweet."
> Judges 14:14b

The riddle was about the lion and honey. Samson wasn't just breaking God's law, he was joking about it for sport. Could it be that Samson's guilty conscience and self-destructive pride wouldn't let him forget what he'd done?

He would have been better off staying silent. But if there's anything else we learn about Samson, he just didn't know when to shut up! Especially when a beautiful woman was involved.

For three days the men were stumped, and on the fourth day they went to Samson's new wife with their frustrations. They demanded she get the answer, "or we will burn you and your father's household to death." (Judges 14:15) What a horrific spot this woman found herself in, but rather than going to her new husband with the truth she decided to betray him. Did she already view him as untrustworthy? Was she simply more committed to her own people than to Samson, part of God's warning against the dangers of intermarriage?

When she pressed for the riddle's solution Samson reminded his new bride that he hadn't even told his parents, so she decided to cry . . . for seven days straight. He caved and told her, she told the Philistines, and they returned to Samson with the answer. Then things really went off the rails:

Then the Spirit of the LORD came powerfully upon him. He went down to Ashkelon, struck down thirty of their men, stripped them of everything and gave their clothes to those who had explained the riddle. Burning with anger, he returned to his father's home. And Samson's wife was given to one of his companions who had attended him at the feast.

Judges 14:19–20

But this story is not over just yet, not by a long shot.

Samson went back to his father-in-law's home, bearing the gift of a goat, and asked to go to his wife. Yes, the one who had completely betrayed him. His father-in-law not only told Samson he couldn't see her, but revealed she had indeed been given away to one of his companions. As you might expect at this point in the story, Samson lost it.

> So he went out and caught three hundred foxes and tied them tail to tail in pairs. He then fastened a torch to every pair of tails, lit the torches and let the foxes loose in the standing grain of the Philistines. He burned up the shocks and standing grain, together with the vineyards and olive groves.
>
> **Judges 15:4–5**

Once the Philistines discovered it was Samson, they took the brutal step of burning his wife and her father to death (Judges 15:6). How devastated he must have been at that point. Far beyond just the grief over a broken marriage, Samson had to confront the horrific murders of two people who had just become family to him. Did he also bear the burden of guilt over their barbarous killings? Whatever emotions he was experiencing he channeled into rage.

Samson vowed revenge. We're told he "viciously" slaughtered many Philistines, then went to hide out in a cave (Judges 15:8). It's hard to think of a more inauspicious beginning to a "love story" than what Samson experienced, and many people don't even know this early part of his story. As he was stewing in that cave, the Philistines went up into Judah looking for him.

Then three thousand men from Judah went down to the cave in the rock of Etam and said to Samson, "Don't you realize that the Philistines are rulers over us? What have you done to us?"

He answered, "I merely did to them what they did to me."

They said to him, "We've come to tie you up and hand you over to the Philistines."

Samson said, "Swear to me that you won't kill me yourselves."

Judges 15:11–12

The people of Judah were so afraid of their merciless oppressors that they immediately went to find and hand over the one man who had shown any degree of strength against their domination. Samson agreed to let his own people bind him and turn him over to his enemies. As the Philistines approached to take him, the Spirit of the Lord again came over him. We're told he took up the jawbone of a donkey and "struck down a thousand men." (Judges 15:15) Samson then led, or judged, the nation of Israel for twenty years.

That's enough drama to make for an entire lifetime, but we haven't even gotten to the most famous part of Samson's life: his relationship with Delilah. And what does all this backstory have to do with that affair? Well, a lot. He had plenty of baggage by the time he met Delilah. We, like Samson, take our life experiences into each new relationship. That's true even when we desperately want a fresh, new start. Samson was shaped by the grief of the loss of his first wife, and by the violence and betrayal of that relationship. We know he was impulsive and angry, prone to immature moods and self-destructive theatrics. We've also learned that his weakness was the temptation of his eyes, of the flesh. The primary thing that mattered to Samson was whatever he judged to be right in his own eyes.

And yet God was still able to use him. The happiness of Samson's childhood, and the grief of his youth, were both long behind him by the time he met Delilah. He was a seasoned warrior and leader, but his weakness for women was still very apparent. At the start of Judges 16, before Delilah entered the picture, Samson slept with a prostitute. It led to yet another moment when his enemies thought they had surrounded him, vowing to kill him (Judges 16:2). Instead, he escaped and ripped out the city gates and the posts holding them and carried them away.

Some would simply label Samson's problem "lust," and while they wouldn't necessarily be wrong, that word might not fully capture what Samson was really after. When someone goes from one flawed relationship to another, we have to consider what gaping hole of emptiness they may be trying to fill. Was Samson hoping to find what his parents had? Did he keep searching in the hopes he would find a woman like his mother to "complete" him.

The Bible tells us that Samson "fell in love" with Delilah (Judges 16:4). This is the first time we see the word "love" used to describe one of Samson's relationships. But what she felt in return is the more important question because it didn't take long for her to stab him in the back when the right offer came along.

The rulers of the Philistines went to her and said, "See if you can lure him into showing you the secret of his great strength and how we can overpower him so we may tie

him up and subdue him. Each one of us will give you eleven hundred shekels of silver."
Judges 16:5

Samson had wreaked such havoc on the Philistines that their leaders were willing to pay handsomely to overtake him.

This is also where I start to question whether he resembled Fabio at all. He was able to perform superhuman feats of strength and destruction with his bare hands, yet everyone seemed confused about how he was able to do such things. Could it be that he just looked like an average guy with a man bun ... who sometimes turned into The Hulk? In any case, his enemies wanted answers and they planned to use a manipulative woman to get them.

Delilah was pretty blunt, making Samson's eventual downfall even more surprising. She didn't sneak around hoping to stumble upon his secret. Nope. She went straight to him and asked the source of his strength *and* how he could be subdued. Not subtle. Three times he lied to her, and each time Delilah revealed exactly what she was up to. She had tried the methods Samson told her would disable him, only to watch him easily break free. Then she had the gall to lecture him about not really being in love with her and making her look like a fool. The obvious question seems to be: a fool to whom? *Delilah, who's taking note of your attempts to destroy me and mocking you when they don't work?*

Why didn't Samson end things with Delilah after the first betrayal? The second? The third? Those are the kinds of questions you may have asked someone you love who's in an unhealthy or abusive relationship. *How can you keep trusting yourself to this person? Don't you see the problem here?* You may feel frustration if it appears they're incapable of walking away.

You may be reading Samson's story and shouting: *Get up! Walk out the door! Leave Delilah and don't look back!* Her actions proved she didn't love Samson and clearly didn't have his best interests at heart. Sometimes it can be difficult for us to recognize when the usual gender dynamics are reversed, but there is no question that Samson was in a manipulative and abusive relationship.

What about Samson's relationship with God? Step by step it seems he's been abandoning the strict Nazirite vow his parents committed him to, as the Lord had commanded. Even though it appears Samson had already broken two parts of his Nazirite vow, he seemed hesitant to break this last rule. Was he keeping his unshorn hair, thinking he could cling to God's favor by following that part of the vow, while abusing His mercy in every other way? The truth is, the more we sin the easier it is for those "things we'd never do" to become possible.

Scripture tells us Delilah nagged Samson mercilessly, night and day. He finally told her the truth about his uncut locks. Did he think God would protect him anyway? Was he really unable to handle the manipulations of a pestering woman? Regardless of what he believed would happen when he gave away his secret, the consequences were swift and disastrous. When Samson awoke, his hair shorn, the Lord had left him. There could be nothing more devastating.

We can quickly discover just how weak and helpless we are without God's favor and mercy. That was also the story of Israel, over and over again, throughout the time of the Judges. It's the story of every one of us when we set our hearts on anything other than God. It was Samson's story.

The Philistines easily captured Samson for the first time, gouging his eyes out and taking him prisoner. It appeared to be an unspeakably tragic ending to such a promising life, yet Samson's story was far from over.

Delilah

Samson's background is only part of this story. What about the mysterious woman who caused his utter downfall (with a heavy assist from him, I might add)? If she didn't love him, why was Delilah in a relationship with Samson in the first place? And who was she?

All we know of her is that she was "a woman in the Valley of Sorek whose name was Delilah." (Judges 16:4) The valley was—and still is today—one of the chief drainage basins in the Judean hills, forming part of the border between the Israelite land of the tribe of Dan and the territory of the Philistines. Delilah came from this borderland, but the Bible does not tell us whether she was Jewish or Philistine. We know that Samson's preference seems to have been for Philistine women. On the other hand, Delilah is a Hebrew name. So we don't really know her ethnic or religious identity, and if Samson actually married her or not.

The only things we learn about their relationship are negative. She was approached by Philistine leaders who wanted to get to the bottom of Samson's supernatural strength, and she appeared to be a very willing accomplice. It was a strength that stood as a challenge to the Philistines' oppression of the people of Israel. The earlier exploits of Samson were the adventures of an impetuous young man at various times carried away by lust, violence, pride, rage, and grief. Was that Samson long gone? When Delilah met him, Samson had been a judge over Israel for two decades. We don't know what drew her to Samson. All we can assess Delilah by is her willingness to backstab a man who'd professed his love for her.

Remember, those Philistine leaders had offered her 1,100 shekels of silver from "each one of us." (Judges 16:5) We have no way of knowing how many leaders made the offer to Delilah, but "each one of us" points to more than two. Eleven-hundred shekels would equal roughly 27.5 pounds of silver. Even if there were just three leaders making the deal, she stood to reap more than eighty-two pounds of silver—an unimaginable sum of money for anyone in the ancient world—much less a woman. That's lottery-jackpot money, the kind of money that would change everything, money that ensured a life of luxury usually available only to kings and queens. With that amount of money, anything was possible. Scripture tells us her motivation in black and white: She did it for money.

After her first attempt at delivering Samson into the hands of his enemies, Delilah became noticeably less patient. She called Samson a liar and complained about how she ended up looking foolish. Twice more he lied to her and easily escaped her plans to betray him.

> Then she said to him, "How can you say, 'I love you,' when you won't confide in me? This is the third time you have made a fool of me and haven't told me the secret of your

great strength." With such nagging she prodded him day after day until he was sick to death of it.
Judges 16:15–16

The emotional manipulation was ruthless. Delilah accused Samson not only of a lack of trust, but also of a lack of love. She must have understood what drove him, what weakness made him captive to this defective relationship. And she twisted that to her advantage. Samson finally caved.

So he told her everything. "No razor has ever been used on my head," he said, "because I have been a Nazirite dedicated to God from my mother's womb. If my head were shaved, my strength would leave me, and I would become as weak as any other man."
Judges 16:15–17

And with that the Philistines finally got their man.

Of all the love stories we examine in this book, Samson and Delilah's probably was the worst and most dysfunctional. All relationships have times of testing, times of mutual sorrow, and maybe even times of betrayal. It seems Samson and Delilah didn't have anything but sorrow and betrayal—or if they did, we don't get a glimpse of any happiness that came before their tragic ending. It might be easy to think, *This story has nothing to do with me or my marriage.* But I firmly believe stories are included in God's Holy Word specifically so that we do find the lessons, whether the earthly ending is happy or disastrous.

Samson and Delilah's relationship was corrupted and destroyed by the love of money—Delilah's lust for it. We don't actually know whether this relationship was ever in positive territory. By the time we arrive, it's turned to greed and treachery. All that abuse and manipulation flowed from the corrupting influence of the bribe that Delilah took and the deception that dirty money required her to practice.

In the New Testament, Paul tells us that "the love of money is the root of all kinds of evil." (I Timothy 6:10) What lies behind most worldly attempts to amass more and more money: the desire for control. The love of money can be a kind of gluttony, an insatiable appetite rooted in our need to manage our world and everything that happens to us according to our own desires. The love of money can stem from a lack of trust in God and in God's providence—and in a marriage, a lack of trust in our partner too.

Delilah's head was turned by a life-changing sum of money, all aimed at helping Samson's enemies figure out how to take him down. In the end, the source of his strength wasn't some magic formula. It was the Spirit of God abiding with him as a result of the vow of consecration his parents had made to God on his behalf before he was born. Samson was flippant with his commitment to God, and eventually he threw it away. By revealing the secret of his unshorn hair to Delilah, he showed a cavalier attitude to the holy things of God. Of course, she also bore much of the blame for what happened to Samson. Their relationship was a cascade of one sin after another, and Samson's lifelong rebellious spirit led him to betray his vow to God by treating it so lightly.

Where did he wind up? Bound and blinded. Isn't that what sin does to all of us? It promises exhilaration, fulfillment, and adventure—and it may provide that for a season. In the end, however, we are its slave. Just as Samson wound up a defeated prisoner of the Philistines, so sin will ultimately render us broken and captive. God doesn't want our hearts to be beholden to anything but Him, and He is always waiting to redeem us from the jail of our mistakes. It only requires that we call to him for help, just as Samson did one final time.

God did not forget Samson when the once-great warrior reached out to him in the midst of utter despair and humiliation. Toward the end of Judges 16 we find the Philistines giving their false god, Dagon, the credit for delivering Samson into their hands.

> "Our god has delivered our enemy into our hands,
>   the one who laid waste our land
>   and multiplied our slain."
> While they were in high spirits, they shouted, "Bring out Samson to entertain us." So they called Samson out of the prison, and he performed for them.
> Judges 16:24b–25a

Samson was reduced to being a freakshow at a party celebrating his undoing, but the fallen hero had a plan.

> When they stood him among the pillars, Samson said to the servant who held his hand, "Put me where I can feel the pillars that support the temple, so that I may lean against them." Now the temple was crowded with men and women; all the rulers of the Philistines were there, and on the roof were about three thousand men and women watching Samson perform.
> Judges 16:26b–27

Samson was ready to punish the Philistines by laying down his own life, but he knew he couldn't do it without the return of God's blessing on his efforts. He started off by clearly recognizing and calling out on the one true God, the God of his people.

> Then Samson prayed to the LORD, "Sovereign LORD, remember me. Please, God, strengthen me just once more, and let me with one blow get revenge on the Philistines for my two eyes." Then Samson reached toward the two central pillars on which the temple stood. Bracing himself against them, his right hand on the one and his left hand on the other, Samson said, "Let me die with the Philistines!" Then he pushed with all his might, and down came the temple on the rulers and all the people in it. Thus he killed many more when he died than while he lived.
>
> **Judges 16:28-30**

Samson's eyes had been gouged out by his enemies, yet his redemption came about not despite his blindness but because of it. His entire life, he had behaved in the way that was right in his own eyes. He was dominated by his own lust, his heart drawn along by his sight. It took losing his sight for him to see God clearly.

The chains of Samson's sin were never stronger than the mercy and love of God, and even in Samson's darkness—even when he thought his own bad decisions and relationships may have alienated God from him forever—even then, God was there. Finally, Samson understood just how holy and powerful the Lord was. Blind and weak, he approached God with a humility totally at odds with his formerly cocky self. And he found a victory greater than any he ever achieved in his prideful, rage-fueled massacres.

We even find Samson's story of redemption included in the "Faith Heroes Hall of Fame" as it's often known in Hebrews 11. He's included with Gideon, Barak, Jephthah, David, Samuel, and the prophets:

> who through faith conquered kingdoms, administered justice, and gained what was promised; who shut the mouths of lions, quenched the fury of the flames, and escaped the edge of the sword; whose weakness was turned to strength; and who became powerful in battle and routed foreign armies.
> Hebrews 11:33-34

I can think of no better endorsement of his redemption—and God's unending grace—than Samson's presence on this list of honor.

Prayer: God of heartbreak, forgive me for the times when I have betrayed Your trust in me, and for the times when I have wounded others. Where I have been prideful and selfish, may my heart humbly return to You with repentance and obedience. If trust has been damaged in my marriage, grant us both the grace to commit to each other with renewed hope, for You are the God of restoration and new beginnings.

The Original Love Story

Genesis 1–4

If you spent any time in church growing up, your instruction about the Bible probably started right where the Scriptures do: with Adam and Eve. They are the beginning of human life, the first marriage and the parents of us all. This first couple was probably the launching point for all the Old Testament stories you learned as a child from Noah to David to Jonah. They provide us with so many rich truths about how God designed a perfect world for humanity, with thoughtful details and beautiful wonders. Adam and Eve also show us what happens when our pride drives us to believe we could be equal to God, chasing our own kingdom instead of pursing and furthering His.

I still remember those old Sunday School days, paper Bible figures that stayed tucked away in sturdy envelopes until they were carefully drawn out and placed up on the board to help us to visualize the story of Creation. Boy, did our imaginations get going. I've never liked snakes. In fact, I detest them! And I wonder how much of that traces back to my earliest recollections of the evil, lying serpent in the Garden of Eden. There was also that forbidden fruit and fig leaves hiding all the important body parts—and chatter about people being naked. Even then I got the contrast of a time when people didn't even know they were unclothed and they were perfectly comfortable that way. What kind of world was that? I understood we weren't living in that one anymore.

But the story of Adam and Eve is filled with plenty of spiritual meat we probably can't fathom at five or six. And it's often when we return to the stories of our childhood—or the ones we first read early in our spiritual walk—that we realize there's so much more going on. This story isn't just about talking animals and magical trees; it's about the beauty of relationship and how God's design for a perfect world shifted in an instant.

God begins the whole story of salvation—humanity's journey to God—with a marriage. A man and a woman building a life together, partnered together as the beginning point of everything that comes after. There would be no Noah, David, Jonah, or Jesus if Adam and Eve hadn't found their way through devastating circumstances in order to stick together and launch the rest of humankind. Marriage is not some afterthought to Scripture, but the whole foundation of everything else.

Let's remember, Adam and Eve aren't just symbols, they were actual flesh-and-blood people just like us. Their lives, like ours, were complicated and challenging. Just like every human being who's followed in their footsteps, Adam and Eve were a mixture of good and evil. They didn't begin their existence as sinners, but because of the choices they made—the rest of us do. They were tempted, just as we are. They chose what felt best to them in the moment, shattering a perfect, unblemished relationship with their Heavenly Father. But He ultimately loved all of us so much that He created a way for us to journey back to Him, to spend eternity with Him—rather than separated from Him forever. In Adam and Eve's complex story lie deep and vital lessons about companionship, sin, and what it means to truly know another person.

In the beginning . . .

Genesis 1 brings us the beautiful story of Creation. We watch as God carefully and powerfully shapes one thing after another that leads to everything we know about our existence: day, night, sun, plants, animals, and eventually mankind. We repeatedly see the words "and God saw that it was good" throughout this chapter. Remember that! You'll see why it's important a bit later. Finally at the end of Genesis 1, God crafted His masterpiece:

> Then God said, "Let us make mankind in our image, in our likeness, so that they may rule over the fish in the sea and the birds in the sky, over the livestock and all the wild animals, and over all the creatures that move along the ground."
> So God created mankind in his own image,
> in the image of God he created them;
> male and female he created them.
> Genesis 1:26–27

When the Scripture speaks of God making humans in His image or likeness, it's not the physical body. God is a spiritual being, not confined by our human boundaries. But He clearly made us with a sense of awareness, an ability to reason and make independent choices. We have emotions and logical reasoning. We are distinct from all the plants and animals in those respects. We're capable of a relationship with God, communing with and worshipping Him. And right away we see two things God did for humanity: blessed it and gave it dominion over everything else. With that certainly comes the responsibility to manage it wisely.

In Genesis 2 we get more details about how God created man.

> **Then the LORD God formed a man from the dust of the ground and breathed into his nostrils the breath of life, and the man became a living being.**
> **Genesis 2:7**

Again, we are unique in that God Himself breathed life into us. That didn't happen with the fishes or aardvarks. Nope. Adam was something special and distinct among all of God's creations. We also see that God created the Garden of Eden and placed Adam there.

> **The LORD God made all kinds of trees grow out of the ground—trees that were pleasing to the eye and good for food. In the middle of the garden were the tree of life and the tree of the knowledge of good and evil.**
> **Genesis 2:9**

We'll talk about those trees in just a minute, but note that God didn't just send Adam there to hang out in a hammock. Verse 15 tells us specifically that God placed Adam in the Garden "to work it and take care of it." If you've ever thought—or been taught—

that work is part of God's punishment for us as a result of Adam and Eve's sin, that's just not the case. God gave man a purpose in work. That was part of His original, ideal plan for us.

After God put Adam in that beautiful place and gave him his assignment, He followed that up with some very specific instructions. God told Adam that there were all kinds of tasty, glorious fruits to choose from, but warned him against one tree in particular.

> "... but you must not eat from the tree of the knowledge of good and evil, for when you eat from it you will certainly die."
> Genesis 2:17

Those were the marching orders. There were no exceptions. There were no outs. And right after that, for the first time, we see that God said something was "not good." (v. 18) He was talking about man being alone. He immediately added to that pronouncement, "I will make a helper suitable for him." But before God did that, He had another fun task for Adam—naming every single animal He'd created.

> So the man gave names to all the livestock, the birds in the sky and all the wild animals.
> But for Adam no suitable helper was found.
> Genesis 2:20

Imagine seeing the majestic lions and elephants, along with the furry little field mice and otters. How spectacularly different each one must have seemed. How did Adam decide? This was an enormous responsibility, and God entrusted it to the unique creation He'd just made. Yet after reviewing things of all shapes and sizes, covered in feathers and fur, we see the sad notation that there's not one match in there for Adam. So God made him one.

> So the LORD God caused the man to fall into a deep sleep; and while he was sleeping, he took one of the man's ribs and then closed up the place with flesh. Then the LORD God made a woman from the rib he had taken out of the man, and he brought her to the man.
> Genesis 2:21–22

This time, instead of going to the dust to craft another complex, distinct human being, God created her from Adam's own body. In *Matthew Henry's Commentary on the Whole Bible*, Henry wrote this fascinating observation:

> The woman was made of a rib out of the side of Adam; not made out of his head to rule over him, nor out of his feet to be trampled upon by him, but out of his side to be equal with him, under his arm to be protected, and near his heart to be beloved.[1]

What a delightful way to describe the relationship intended between Adam and Eve. It's easy for us to misunderstand the word "helper." There is no denying that on first reading, Eve comes across as Adam's auxiliary—one who will assist him in the work God has given him. But does that make her any less human or valuable? The answer is unequivocally *no*. If we dig into the Hebrew word Scripture uses for Eve, we discover that the Bible's definition of "helper" may be a bit different from ours.

The word for "helper" in Hebrew is *ezer*. It's a simple word, one used with some frequency in the Bible. At its root, *ezer* means strong or saving. *Ezer* is not just help—it's rescuing. When Moses' second son was born in the land of Midian, he named him Eliezer, which means "my God is my help."

> For [Moses] said, "My father's God was my helper; he saved me from the sword of Pharaoh."
> Exodus 18:4

In the book of the prophet Hosea, God told His people, "You are destroyed, Israel, because you are against me, against your *ezer*." (Hosea 13:9) When Moses at the end of his life asked God's blessing on the tribes of Israel, he implored God about Judah, "Oh, be his *ezer* against his foes!" (Deuteronomy 33:7) And when the psalmist sang of the blessings that befall those who trust only in the Lord, he cried out,

> Blessed are those whose *ezer* is the God of Jacob,
> whose hope is in the LORD their God!
> Psalm 146:4

In fact, in almost every instance when the word *ezer* is used in the Bible, it is used to describe the saving action of God Himself. God is not there to be an assistant! He is there to reach in with His strong right arm and deliver His people, to be the support that will not fail, the strong one who cannot be vanquished. God uses the very same word for Eve that He uses to describe Himself. Can you think of a greater honor to pay to any human being? Somehow "assistant" doesn't seem to be the idea here, does it?

Instead, God intended for the relationship between Adam and Eve to be one in which they could rely on each other in the same way they relied on God. Eve was not God's afterthought, but an essential part of her husband's life and of the plan of creation. To be a "helper" is an incredible mission. And it started out in such a glorious place—both literally and figuratively. Look at Adam's reaction to meeting Eve:

> "This is now bone of my bones
>   and flesh of my flesh;
>   she shall be called 'woman,'
>   for she was taken out of man."
> Genesis 2:23

From the beginning, Adam understood that they were like none other. There was no comparison to the hundreds or thousands of animals he'd examined and named. Eve was literally a part of him. Ephesians 5:28 says "husbands ought to love their wives as their own bodies."

> That is why a man leaves his father and mother and is united to his wife, and they become one flesh.
> Adam and his wife were both naked, and they felt no shame.
> Genesis 2:24–25

These closing verses in Genesis 2 give us great insight into the plan for marriage. Two people leave their loved ones and join together, sharing that same bond that Adam and Eve first had. They were God's cherished creations, in a stunning world filled with purpose and peace. "They felt no shame" in their bodies. What we see here is true intimacy and vulnerability, both physically and emotionally. There was nothing to hide from each other.

Those of us who are married know there are plenty of seasons that aren't about fairy tales, but even in those challenges, when we're bonded to each other in true intimacy we can find great security and comfort. I remember in the early years of our marriage, thinking that my laugh sounded differently than it ever had before. It was more boisterous and less reserved. I know that's an odd observation to make, but I have a memory of thinking it signaled something new and different. It was coming from a place of zero hesitation or self-consciousness. It truly felt as if I had found my person and was safe to live with—and express—all my emotions, good or bad. What Adam and Eve started out with was even more open and pure, not yet touched by sin.

Trouble

If the story of Adam and Eve was a TV show, this is the point you'd hear that scratching sound like a needle skipping across a record. (Some of you may need to Google that.) All that bliss and innocence is about to come to a screeching halt. A serpent, described as more cunning than any other creature God had made, came calling to Eve.

> He said to the woman, "Did God really say, 'You must not
> eat from any tree in the garden'?"
> Genesis 3:1b

Numerous other references in the Bible make clear this is Satan at work. He started with Eve as he often does with us, trying to sow doubt about what God has really commanded. She responded by trying to correct him.

> The woman said to the serpent, "We may eat fruit from
> the trees in the garden, but God did say, 'You must not eat
> fruit from the tree that is in the middle of the garden, and
> you must not touch it, or you will die.'"
> Genesis 3:2-3

Listen up! Be careful when the enemy comes calling. Yes, you can tell Satan he is a liar when he shows up with temptation. Quote Scripture, shout him down. Do not engage with him, as if he is worthy of a reasonable conversation. When we are weak or weary, or simply caught off guard there's nothing more the enemy would like than to try to entangle us in a spiral of doubt and contradictions. Ephesians 4:27 warns, "do not give the devil a foothold." The first chance you get: sweep the leg.

The serpent fired back with a half-truth.

> "You will not certainly die," the serpent said to the woman.
> "For God knows that when you eat from it your eyes will be
> opened, and you will be like God, knowing good and evil."
> Genesis 3:4-5

This is another one of his schemes, tucking a kernel of truth into a bushel of deception. He knew Eve wouldn't immediately, physically, drop dead. He tempted her with the possibility that she could become just like God. Does that sound familiar? He twisted the truth, priming Eve's heart to accept the next big lie.

When the woman saw that the fruit of the tree was good for food and pleasing to the eye, and also desirable for gaining wisdom, she took some and ate it.
Genesis 3:4-6

There is an important lesson for us here, about assuming that we know better than God. Too often a voice inside us says, *Aha, I know what God must be up to here, but I can short-circuit that.* That voice is not from God. Our only job is to trust God's words and to follow His commands, even when—maybe especially when—we don't see the point.

Eve did what we sometimes do: She substituted her own reasoning for God's. She may not have meant, on a conscious level, to rebel against God. It certainly didn't hurt that the fruit looked appetizing. And of course there was that bit about being like God in there, the part the serpent had emphasized. Notice which part came first for her: the sheer pleasure of the thing. At the end of the day, I don't think Eve made a theological decision. She saw something she wanted, and she took it. That sounds familiar to a lot of us, in our own experience with the way sin works. Sin will always tell you that it's no big deal—and besides, it looks so nice and tastes so delicious! The book of James warns us:

... each person is tempted when they are dragged away by their own evil desire and enticed. Then, after desire has conceived, it gives birth to sin; and sin, when it is full-grown, gives birth to death.

James 1:14-15

Sin leads to spiritual death and separation from God, which Adam and Eve would soon discover.

Notice what happened next: Eve immediately turned to Adam and shared the fruit with him.

She also gave some to her husband, who was with her, and he ate it.

Genesis 3:6b

Wait—what? I don't remember hearing it that way in Sunday School or in the pages of my children's picture Bible. Adam was ... standing ... right ... there. Was he with Eve for the whole conversation with the serpent? I'm not sure when Adam walked up, but he was there by the time she decided to take that fruit and eat it. A lot of Christian teaching over the years has put all the blame on Eve for the calamity in the garden, but while she started the ball rolling, Adam is the one Paul later named as the reason that death came into the world (Romans 5:12). Adam's sin was the moment mankind fell. What was going on in his head? We don't know. He certainly didn't protest when Eve handed him the fruit.

He definitely had some thoughts, though, once the two of them got caught! By the time God went to see Adam, his and Eve's eyes had been "opened" and they realized they were naked.

They'd made coverings out of fig leaves, and hid when they heard God coming. When the Lord called out to ask where Adam was, he had an answer ready:

> . . . "I heard you in the garden, and I was afraid because I was naked; so I hid." And he said, "Who told you that you were naked? Have you eaten from the tree that I commanded you not to eat from?" The man said, "The woman you put here with me—she gave me some fruit from the tree, and I ate it."
> Genesis 3:10–12

Oh, okay. Adam not only blamed Eve, he also pointed the finger at God. *You gave me this woman, you know, the one who started this whole thing.* Everything Adam said to God was true—God had given him an *ezer*, a woman to be with him, and then Eve had given him the fruit. But it is shocking how quickly Adam began making the case for how innocent he was in the whole mess.

The Bible doesn't tell us what Eve said to Adam about that, but she took his lead and also began shifting the blame.

> Then the Lord God said to the woman, "What is this you have done?"
> The woman said, "The serpent deceived me, and I ate."
> Genesis 3:13

True, the enemy warped and twisted the truth. However, Adam and Eve had clearly been commanded by God not to eat from that one specific tree. They each allowed themselves to put aside what God had said and believe the serpent's lie so they could pursue their own selfish desires. They each made their own sinful choices, and then they tried to pass the buck. And now they were about to find out just how much it would cost them.

God first leveled a curse on the serpent, and foreshadowed what would be his ultimate defeat by Christ and the plan of salvation. That, God may have relished. But I wonder if his heart was broken as He then explained to Adam and Eve how drastically their idyllic lives would change.

> To the woman he said,
> > "I will make your pains in childbearing very severe;
> > with painful labor you will give birth to children.
> > Your desire will be for your husband,
> > and he will rule over you."
> > Genesis 3:16

And for Adam, no more of the peaceful life he'd first known in Eden:

> "Cursed is the ground because of you;
> > through painful toil you will eat food from it
> > all the days of your life.
> > It will produce thorns and thistles for you,
> > and you will eat the plants of the field.
> > By the sweat of your brow
> > you will eat your food
> > until you return to the ground,
> > since from it you were taken;

for dust you are
and to dust you will return."
Genesis 3:17b–19

Adam's work would become toilsome and difficult, and then he would die—returning to the very dust God had used to create him.

Once Adam and Eve had acquired the knowledge of good and evil, God noted they couldn't stay in the Garden and eat from the Tree of Life. It would give them immortality if they ate from it. Instead, they were banished from Eden and a cherubim with a flaming sword stood there to guard the Tree from the two people who could not be trusted to obey God's commands. Such a painful sentence: banished from the only world they'd ever known, with the knowledge they were going to die. Death entered creation through Adam.

The loss of their home, the world as they knew it, and their divine purpose was not the end of tragedy in Adam and Eve's lives. They faced heartbreak as parents too. When you read the story of Cain murdering his brother Abel, it's easy to miss how devastating this must have been for Adam and Eve. They had obviously raised the two to understand the importance of offering sacrifices to God. But when they did so on one particular occasion, God favored Abel's over Cain's—and that made Cain very angry (Genesis 4:3–5).

The Lord confronted Cain:

Then the LORD said to Cain, "Why are you angry? Why is your face downcast? If you do what is right, will you not be accepted? But if you do not do what is right, sin

is crouching at your door; it desires to have you, but you must rule over it."
Genesis 4:6-7

Instead, Cain lured Abel into a field and killed him—then played dumb.

Then the LORD said to Cain, "Where is your brother Abel?" "I don't know," he replied. "Am I my brother's keeper?"
Genesis 4:9

The consequences were swift and devastating. God told Cain he would be under a curse, no longer able to cultivate crops from the land and would live as a "restless wanderer on the earth." (Genesis 4:10)

In this punishment, Adam and Eve lost two sons at once. Did they feel they'd failed as parents? Whatever lessons they had tried to teach Cain about the importance of controlling his own emotions—let alone the importance of human life—had not been heeded. Cain's sin was not unlike Eve's sin in that way. Both of them brushed aside what they knew to be right because they were overcome by the emotion of the moment: desire and greed on the part of Eve, while rage and resentment drove Cain.

Recovery

So where did all this leave Adam and Eve? What happened to their relationship, in the wake of not just one, but two unimaginable tragedies? As a result of the Fall, Adam and Eve were banished from the only world they'd ever known. Plus, they had to live with the knowledge that their mistake had lasting, cosmic consequences. How does a marriage survive that?

Two things happened in the immediate aftermath of their first tragedy. Scripture tells us that Adam gave Eve a new name, and they made love as husband and wife. Remember, when Eve was first presented to Adam, he named her "woman," saying that "she shall be called woman, for she was taken out of man." (Genesis 2:23) The Hebrew word in this verse is *ishah,* closely related to the word for man, *ish.* The man and woman were two halves of a whole, two parts of the same word.

After the loss of Eden, Adam gave his wife a new name: "Adam named his wife Eve, because she would become the mother of all the living." (Genesis 3:20) "Eve" (from the Latin "Eva") is our English form of her Hebrew name, *Chava.* This name shares a root with the verb that means "being" or "existing." It makes a kind of logical sense—obviously as the first woman on earth, she would be the mother of everyone else. Was Adam trying to ease Eve's pain, by giving her a new outlook along with her new name? Her first title or label, *ishah,* pointed back to Adam, and to her relationship with him. Her new name, *Chava,* pointed her forward. Yes, she was still "bone of [his] bones and flesh of his flesh." But Eve was the one who would take that bone and flesh and from them create the whole human race—everyone who has ever existed, or will exist, descends from this complicated, imperfect, beloved woman. *You are larger than just me,* Adam seemed to be saying in giving her this name. *You still have a purpose, and a mission.* Even more important, it's a mission Adam shared with her.

The second thing Adam did was to make love to his wife. Other translations say things like "had relations with" (New American Standard Bible) or "was intimate with" (New English Bible). But none of those is really an accurate reflection of the Hebrew word, which is a strange one. The good old-fashioned King James Bible that many of us grew up with translated it literally: "Adam *knew* Eve his wife." (Genesis 4:1) When the Bible talks about physical intimacy, it relies on the language of knowledge. What does it mean to say that Adam and Eve *knew* each other?

The Hebrew word for "know"—*yadá*—is based on the kind of knowledge we get by seeing something. It stands in contrast to simply learning about a topic or a person in a book. It's the kind of knowledge that comes from living and experiencing something. To know someone in that sense is not just to be acquainted with the *idea* of who they are. To know someone in the *yadá* sense of the word is to really *see* them, at every level and in every way. Adam and Eve did not just experience physical union; they experienced a deep mutual knowledge born of understanding who the other really was as a person.

Maybe we've missed the mark in communicating this wholly unique and special facet of marriage to young people. To really know someone intimately isn't just about having sex with them. It's about that true vulnerability and honesty that Adam and Eve started out with in the Garden of Eden. The biblical plan for sex is one of profound intimacy and mutual knowledge. The fact is, it takes some level of emotional and spiritual maturity to have the ability and capacity to know others deeply—and to let them experience you in that same way.

It's the work of a lifetime, and it isn't something we can do with more than one person at a time, or just casually whenever we feel like it. Monogamy is baked into the idea of that kind of deep, intimate knowledge. Christians wait for marriage, because the *yadá* knowledge of a spouse within the marriage covenant takes time, space, and commitment.

As humans, we will struggle to get these things right. But when we have a goal to aim for, knowing there's something incredible waiting for us there—we can learn to make the effort. It isn't just about avoiding something that's so tempting and intoxicating. Honestly, that can be incredibly tough! But it's about appreciating the amazing things that can happen when you follow God's design.

Twice in their lives, Adam and Eve faced unthinkable sorrow. Twice, they reached for each other in response to that sorrow: once, after they had lost Eden, and again, after they had lost Cain and Abel. After those sons were gone, the Bible tells us that "Adam made love to his wife again, and she gave birth to a son and named him Seth." (Genesis 4:25) What we see in the life of Adam and Eve is a pattern: of togetherness, of rebuilding after terrible events that threatened to pull them apart and destroy them.

Thousands of years later, one of Adam and Eve's descendants would also be totally alone in a different garden, a painful parallel to Adam's early state. In the Garden of Gethsemane this Man whom Paul called "the last Adam" (1 Corinthians 15:45), was abandoned by His friends and family, despite begging for their support in His hour of need. That Man—Jesus—who was also fully God, would then go on to do what His forefather Adam could not: crush the serpent to save humanity.

Adam and Eve fell far short of their potential, but their impact did not end with the Fall. We should view it not only as the story of original sin, but also as the birthplace of original love. One thing's for sure: The story of Adam and Eve is not done teaching us yet.

Prayer: Gracious God, Lord of all love, help me to fully appreciate the beauty of Your original plan for humanity. Please open my eyes to the folly of chasing my own kingdom, thinking I know better than Your divine wisdom. Let those who seek marriage do so with reverence and humility, with a true commitment to know and be known. Wrap Your arms of protection around us and forgive us when we disobey. Increase our love for You, and our love for each other.

JOSEPH AND MARY

A Bond of Trust

Matthew 1:18–2:23, Luke 2:41–52

As I sit typing, sipping my decaf peppermint mocha latte, I'm itching to deck my house out for Christmas. I've *been* ready, so the debate is ongoing with my husband about getting everything down from the attic. Sure, it's not even Thanksgiving yet, but I've got a yearning for the hopeful message of Christ's arrival. It puts the trials of this world in perspective and reminds me of the cherished celebrations of my childhood. Twinkling lights, glittering trees, and baubles—they all fill me with joy. But nothing means more to me than the two nativity displays given to me by people I loved and who have gone on to heaven.

The first is an exact copy of the one my Grandma Nell used to put out every year. It's got a wooden stable and small porcelain figures I move again and again until I've got them perfectly placed. There's even a little moss and hay that seems to multiply and spread wherever I put this treasured display. Over the years I commented many times about how much I loved my grandmother's nativity set when she was still alive. So one year she ordered one for me from the same place she got hers: the Sears and Roebuck Christmas Wish Book. The second is completely different, a delicate collection of ivory china figurines from my late stepmother, Linda. She knew how much I loved the holiday, and I will always treasure her thoughtful gift.

Each year I gingerly unpack the pieces of these two nativity sets and put baby Jesus right in the center, exactly where He belongs. And while He will always be the most important part of the Christmas story, there's so much beauty tucked into the secondary story of Joseph and Mary as a couple. I've often wondered what Joseph's life must have been like, raising a son who wasn't his but who was to be the Savior of the world. Both he and Mary were thrust into a shockingly unexpected journey, and one that would have been much rockier if they hadn't been unified in their faith and trust of each other—and in God's ultimate plan. The Lord of heaven and earth chose to live and grow as a human child as a member of their family, in their home. We know that He must have seen something truly extraordinary in these two ordinary people in first-century Israel.

Unlike many of the relationships described in the Bible, and in this book, there isn't a single negative word about Mary and Joseph's marriage. We see them as honorable people, devoted to each other through some exceptionally difficult circumstances. It's a love story filled with sacrificial love and selflessness, a model that stands the test of time.

The Early Days

One of the first things we learn about Joseph is how he cared for Mary and her reputation. He's called a righteous man, albeit one placed in a rather tricky situation.

This is how the birth of Jesus the Messiah came about: His mother Mary was pledged to be married to Joseph, but before they came together, she was found to be pregnant through the Holy Spirit. Because Joseph her husband was faithful to the law, and yet did not want to expose her to public disgrace, he had in mind to divorce her quietly.

Matthew 1:18–19

What we discover from this passage is that Mary knew she was pregnant, and the news had been shared with Joseph. Joseph knew that people were sure to gossip and talk about her pregnancy outside of marriage—and probably speculate about him too! More important, he knew that her life and well-being would be at risk if she were exposed as an adulterer who had cheated on her betrothed husband. Under the law it would have been considered adultery if Mary had slept with another man. Bottom line, she could have been stoned to death. What must have run through Joseph's mind? Whatever his emotions, he wanted to resolve the situation "quietly" so as not to "expose her to public disgrace."

Joseph's actions were honorable. If you thought you had been betrayed in this way, would you have the strength to act with such dignity? When we've been hurt by someone, our fleshly impulse is often to retaliate. Joseph could have turned the full spotlight of Nazareth's social shame onto young Mary. We all know people—and I can think of one wronged celebrity spouse in particular—who loudly and publicly drag their partner through the mud. Hey, we may think they're justified! Instead, thinking of Mary, Joseph chose to spare her the public ridicule and have a quiet divorce.

What a relevant, important lesson for us today, when just about everything we do is one social media post away from a huge audience. Social media can be an amazing gift, allowing us to stay connected to the people we value, and remain in the lives of so many people we care about. But there's no denying that one of the biggest pitfalls of social media is the way it can wind up shattering someone's life—whether through their own foolish actions or by the concerted effort of someone else to target and destroy them. It's also designed in many ways for us to directly compare our lives with others, an unrealistic standard when so much of what we see is photoshopped to the point it loses any link to reality. We are constantly being reminded that we have to measure up not only in comparison to people we know, but also to complete strangers.

Almost no one posts their marital troubles on social media. "We fought about money again," doesn't have quite the same ring to it as, "Look at our incredible vacation!"

Okay, but what does any of this have to do with Joseph and Mary? First, it's good to remember that even if social media has intensified our fear of what other people might think of our failures, we aren't the only people in history who worried about things like that. Joseph did too! When he was engaged to Mary and then discovered she was pregnant, "What will people think of her?" was among his first thoughts.

God sent a messenger to reassure Joseph.

But after he had considered this, an angel of the LORD appeared to him in a dream and said, "Joseph son of David, do not be afraid to take Mary home as your wife, because what is conceived in her is from the Holy Spirit. She will

give birth to a son, and you are to give him the name Jesus, because he will save his people from their sins."

All this took place to fulfill what the LORD had said through the prophet: "The virgin will conceive and give birth to a son, and they will call him Immanuel" (which means "God with us").

Matthew 1:20–23

The angel's initial reveal to Mary of her blessed role in salvation rightly gets much of the focus in the Christmas story, but God knew Joseph would be an earthly father to His Son and made sure he was also divinely guided and comforted. It's mind-blowing to think of an angel coming to you in a prophetic dream, but imagine also realizing you are going to be a part of the very prophecy you have long studied and awaited as a faithful Jewish man!

The angel told Joseph not to be afraid. It's a message God gives us over and over in Scripture. He knows us well enough to understand that we are going to be fearful. Joseph likely had the fear of the known—that people would disbelieve him and Mary and assume that something sinful had led to her pregnancy. But did Joseph also suffer from a fear of the unknown, as we so often do? Was he worried about abandoning the plans he and Mary had made for this new life turned upside down? What would this heavenly assignment mean to them? Their families? The Jewish people? He would soon be raising the Messiah, the One promised to save them all. We don't know anything about what Joseph had hoped for in his marriage to Mary. We don't know what Mary was hoping for or expecting out of her engagement to Joseph or what her dreams for her marriage might have been before the day that Gabriel showed up. She was a simple, peasant girl from a small village. Neither one could have dreamed they'd be raising the Son of God!

The angel's message to be unafraid in the midst of an unexpected curveball can also apply to our relationships today. *Don't be afraid,* God says to us, *to let go of your dreams about what your marriage will look like.* We hold so tightly to what we think our lives "should" look like, and what we hope our marriage will become. When our relationship deviates from that path, we can be rattled. Sheldon and I couldn't have known when we fell in love that he would be diagnosed with a brain tumor or that both our fathers would die rather suddenly. But none of that was a surprise to our Heavenly Father. He partners together with us in our marriages, guiding us through the painful valleys and strengthening us as partners to our spouses when they are suffering. That can be the exact moment when God is most active in our marriages, and when God's plan is working itself out in our lives together.

Take note of something else the angel told Joseph: "You are to give him the name Jesus." Focus for a minute on the first part of that sentence: "*You* are to give him the name Jesus." What was happening to Mary wasn't just happening to her alone—it was happening to her husband too, to both of them. By making it clear to Joseph that he too had a role (a crucial one, in Jewish tradition) in the birth of this child, the angel was telling Joseph that this was a partnership. The annunciation didn't just happen to Mary; it happened to Joseph too. It happened to their marriage.

Those of us who have been married for a while realize that every momentous event that happens to one partner also happens to the other—the loss of a job, an unexpected promotion, the death of a parent, a surprise honor. That's also true of spiritual highs and lows. When valleys and mountaintops are a part of spiritual lives, our partners are joined with us in that journey. We are one flesh. Joseph, blindsided by all of this miraculous news about the ordinary girl from Nazareth he thought he knew, might have felt like he had no part in it. God made sure he knew that wasn't the case.

Joseph acted on all that was commanded of him.

> ... he did what the angel of the LORD had commanded him and took Mary home as his wife. But he did not consummate their marriage until she gave birth to a son. And he gave him the name Jesus.
> Matthew 1:24b–25

By naming the child Jesus, Joseph became his father in the eyes of Jewish law. According to customs of the day, when the father named a child he was claiming it as a member of his family. In becoming Jesus' earthly father, Joseph was also officially making Him part of the lineage of David. That affiliation came through Joseph's tribal affiliation.

It's true today, as it was centuries ago, that blended families can be a beautiful thing. Like many of you reading this book, I've got a very complicated family tree. My parents divorced when I was young, but I was incredibly blessed to have two kind, loving stepparents in my life. It must have taken a lot for these adults to welcome in a daughter who wasn't theirs, often put together with siblings who may not have wanted a new sister! But much like Joseph, they stepped up to the challenge and agreed to raise me just like one of their own. My stepfather was particularly sensitive to the appearance that he would attempt to take my dad's place in any way. While he was happy to teach me to ride a bike and sit through my piano recitals, my stepdad also wanted to be clear that he would never try to replace my dad. Joseph must have considered those things in his heart and mind as well—how to raise an honorable young man who was actually someone else's son.

Note also that Mary and Joseph followed God's command not to consummate their marriage until after Jesus' birth. That was in keeping with the prophecy that a virgin would give birth to the Messiah. We are called to purity in the face of passion, and there are times when that may even be true within a marriage. Paul writes in the New Testament, after telling husbands and wives to give each other affection and sexual attention:

> **Do not deprive each other except perhaps by mutual consent and for a time, so that you may devote yourselves to prayer.**
> **1 Corinthians 7:5a**

He notes that there can be times our spiritual focus demands all our energy, but he warns spouses against abstaining for too long. Mary and Joseph once again modeled integrity and obedience in their marriage as they awaited the Savior.

Facing Challenges, Together

In addition to the knowledge that they were parenting the Son of God, Mary and Joseph had the practical family tasks of raising other children and building a family and home. I love that the Bible gives us a glimpse into some very real things they experienced in their journey together as parents. It reminds us that they walked through trauma and had to place gut-level trust in what God directed them to do. It's not uncommon for marriages to splinter apart in the midst of stress and trials. When we're in pain or stretched to our breaking points, we can feel isolated and overwhelmed. We can sometimes view our spouses as part of the problem, rather than leaning on them as a source of strength. Ecclesiastes 4 paints a beautiful picture of working together, and I'm always touched when it's read at a wedding.

> Two are better than one,
> because they have a good return for their labor:
> If either of them falls down,
> one can help the other up.
> But pity anyone who falls
> and has no one to help them up.
> Also, if two lie down together, they will keep warm.
> But how can one keep warm alone?
> Though one may be overpowered,
> two can defend themselves.
> A cord of three strands is not quickly broken.
> Ecclesiastes 4:9–12

Not only do we gather strength and hope from each other, but when God is that third strand in our marriages we are reinforced by something far beyond our human abilities. Joseph and Mary discovered that together.

Few of us will ever face the kinds of deadly threats and

upheaval they did. In Matthew 2, we watch as they flee the murderous King Herod who was determined to find and execute Jesus. That required them to abandon all they knew and loved and make a midnight dash to a completely foreign land, with a baby in tow.

> . . . an angel of the LORD appeared to Joseph in a dream. "Get up," he said, "take the child and his mother and escape to Egypt. Stay there until I tell you, for Herod is going to search for the child to kill him." So he got up, took the child and his mother during the night and left for Egypt, where he stayed until the death of Herod. And so was fulfilled what the LORD had said through the prophet: "Out of Egypt I called my son."
>
> Matthew 2:13–15

There was no send-off party or opportunity to lovingly pack up and protect whatever earthly goods or sentimental family treasures they may have cherished. The journey to Egypt was not a short one, and the young couple likely had to stay there for an extended period of time. What was it like for the two of them, in a strange country where they knew no one? Certainly it was an existence unlike any they had known before, and their sense of alienation must have been profound at times. When couples lose everything—home, country, security—they often lose each other too. But it could be that there in Egypt, in that time of trial, was where their marriage became more than just two people united in doing God's will and in keeping the Messiah safe. It might have been a time of bonding as they relied on each other in this distant land, far from their families.

I'm a big fan of the "leave and cleave" idea, but I know it's difficult for some young couples. Often, you may start out actually living with your in-laws as you get through school or save up for a home. But I think there's great wisdom in the idea that you have to leave the nest and build your own life together as husband and wife. A few months after we got married, I graduated from law school and Sheldon and I moved several hours away from my family. We were already separated by several states from the Breams. We had so much to learn about stretching our budget, finding community with other young couples, and managing schedules and expectations. On a daily basis, we only had each other. But what an adventure it was! We found we could actually feed ourselves on less than $50 a week—if we didn't mind eating lots of sandwiches and pasta—and never going out to dinner. We made lots of mistakes, but we were in it together. I imagine Mary and Joseph having some of those same growing pains in the early years of their marriage.

Their young marriage was resilient and it endured. Their love story helps us to reflect on contrasts and connections with other relationships throughout the Bible—especially that of Adam and Eve. Just as the Old Testament began with the story of a marriage, so does the New Testament. The old creation began with a family, and the new creation began with one too. With that parallel in mind, we can see some key things about the union between Joseph and Mary. Like Adam and Eve, they lost the only home they had ever known, forced to flee abruptly and without warning. The overarching circumstances might be similar, but there was a crucial difference in the way that each couple approached their problems. Remember what Adam said when things looked bleak for him and Eve? Adam blamed his partner for his misery:

"The woman you put here with me—she gave me some fruit from the tree, and I ate it." (Genesis 3:12)

Joseph could have said, "Wait just a minute. I've gone along with everything I've been told to do so far, but now I'm supposed to leave my home and everything I've ever known, and flee in the middle of the night like a criminal?" Joseph could have viewed Mary as the one responsible for what ultimately led to them being in that position of danger when Herod was seeking to kill Jesus. But unlike Adam, Joseph didn't point any fingers. He didn't protest, and he didn't separate himself from Mary by suggesting their situation was someone else's problem. Within this marriage we never see anyone playing the blame game.

Why did Joseph take a different path than Adam? There may be a clue in the very first description of Mary's future husband that Scripture gives us. He is described in Matthew 1:19 as *dikaios,* a Greek word with various interpretations. One translation of the word is "faithful to the law," but it actually goes beyond that. It's the same word that is translated elsewhere in the Bible as "righteous." But both of those translations only illustrate a part of the full meaning of this complicated word. Yes, following God's commandments is one part of being *dikaios,* and so is rightness with God and with one's fellow men. But at its root, *dikaios* means something more like "fair, even, equal, well-balanced." One of the oldest uses of the word describes a chariot that is stabilized on all sides: an *arma dikaion* can traverse rough terrain without difficulty because all its wheels are equal and balanced.

In the same way, a person who is *dikaios* could be viewed as someone capable of synthesizing information relevant to a situation and then making a wise, equitable pronouncement. The idea of "balance" is central to the word, helping us to see why

Joseph didn't blame Mary, and why their marriage was a successful one—able to navigate all the rocky terrain they faced. When Adam blamed Eve for what happened, he expressed only one side of the story: the one that made him out to be less at fault. He ignored the reality—that he didn't protest or raise any questions when Eve gave him the fruit. By comparison, Joseph looks like a very different husband under pressure. Rather than leaving his wife to fend for herself in the midst of a disaster, Joseph worked in tandem with Mary. They moved together in obeying God's commands and protecting their family.

Years later, we get another glimpse of Joseph and Mary operating as a team, in the face of a terrifying situation. They had returned from Egypt and settled into a life in Nazareth. He worked as a carpenter, while she focused on their growing family. We get some indication that their family was prospering, as they were able to travel every year for the festival of Passover. In those times, it's unlikely that more modest families would have been able to leave their homes and businesses for a week of travel and lodging. It seems their lives had changed a great deal since their escape and temporary exile in Egypt. But on one of those special trips Joseph and Mary experienced every parent's worst nightmare.

After the festival was over, while his parents were returning home, the boy Jesus stayed behind in Jerusalem, but they were unaware of it. Thinking he was in their company, they traveled on for a day. Then they began looking for him among their relatives and friends. When they did not find him, they went back to Jerusalem to look for him. After three days they found him in the temple courts, sitting among the teachers, listening to them and asking them questions. Everyone who heard him was amazed at his understanding and his answers. When his parents saw him, they were astonished. His mother said to him, "Son, why have you treated us like this? Your father and I have been anxiously searching for you."

Luke 2:43–48

There is so much to unpack here, beginning with the incredible fear that Mary and Joseph must have experienced. The torment of wondering where their son was lasted not for minutes, but for days. The opportunities to blame each other, "Weren't you watching Him?" "No, you told me *you* were watching Him!" must have been many and frequent. Those three days had to have been filled with panic, and likely felt much longer than just seventy-two hours. The temptation to turn on each other—to assign blame—would have been easy to give in to. But notice what Mary said when she found Jesus: "Son, why have you treated *us* like this?"

Here we see that Joseph wasn't the only one working to make this marriage a true partnership. Mary could easily have said, "Why have you treated *me* like this?" What mother would blame her? It would have been natural, in that kind of pain and confusion, when she had believed her child was gone forever, to focus only on her own grief. But Mary didn't do that. She kept the focus on *us,* and she made a point of saying *us* to her son: to *their* son. She went on to say, "Your father and I have been anxiously searching for you." Not only did she express their true partnership by saying *us* even in the midst of her conflicted emotions, but she also mentioned Joseph's grief before her own. She could have said, "We have been anxiously searching for you," but she made a slightly different choice. She explicitly referred to Joseph as "your father."

What does this show us? For one thing, it clearly illustrates that Mary rejected any idea or perception that Jesus was her child alone. Yes, the angel Gabriel appeared to her and greeted her as the one full of grace, and yes, Jesus' birth—and the whole Christian story—features Mary's heavenly assignment. But Jesus also had a real, earthly father, who loved Him and sacrificed and worked to help raise Him. Even as Jesus sat among the teachers and elders in the Temple, soaking up their wisdom and expounding His own as one of them, Mary did not want Him to forget about that other father. Joseph had protected Him and kept Him safe for all those years. Mary stopped to consider how Joseph must have been feeling in the grips of their panic. By her choice of words—"Your father and I"—Mary knitted their family together in a critical moment.

What beautiful lessons we see in Mary and Joseph's marriage about how to encounter grief and tragedy. They were unwavering in their support of each other—in Bethlehem, and in Jerusalem. We witness them opting not to assign blame or put themselves first as individuals. Instead they listened to God—together. They became an unbreakable *us*.

Aloneness and Widowhood

We don't have many details from the Bible about what happened to Mary and Joseph as a couple after Jesus grew into adulthood. We do get one clue in the Gospel of John when we see Jesus in agony on the cross. He specifically entrusted His mother to the care of the apostle John:

> Near the cross of Jesus stood his mother, his mother's sister, Mary the wife of Clopas, and Mary Magdalene. When Jesus saw his mother there, and the disciple whom he loved standing nearby, he said to her, "Woman, here is your son," and to the disciple, "Here is your mother." From that time on, this disciple took her into his home.
> John 19:25–27

If Joseph had still been alive, Jesus would not have appointed someone other than Joseph to care for Mary. It would appear that Joseph had passed away by the time Jesus was losing his own earthly life on the cross. It is probable that Joseph died before Jesus began His public ministry, because at various points in that ministry His mother traveled with Him and His disciples. It is unlikely that Mary would have left her husband alone. Was Joseph's death some sort of catalyst for the beginning of Jesus' earthly ministry? Scripture doesn't tell us. All we know is that at the end, Mary was alone again. It's interesting to note that, as some point out, God may have entrusted His greatest treasure, His son, to the care of a single mother. I know just how resourceful and faithful they can be because of the tenacity and humility my mom showed during the period she was raising me on her own.

The vast majority of all married couples face this kind of separation Mary and Joseph did—when one spouse dies before the other. Just as Mary and Joseph showed us how to walk the path of pain, challenge, and difficulty in their marriage—finding new ways to forge togetherness in the process—Mary also modeled strength in widowhood. Not only was she present in the most unimaginably horrible moment of losing her son, but she continued to show up at the core of the early church—even as early believers faced the continuous threat of losing their lives. In Acts 1 we find her gathered with the apostles after Jesus' death and Resurrection.

> **They all joined together constantly in prayer, along with the women and Mary the mother of Jesus, and with his brothers.**
> Acts 1:14

My late mother-in-law, Jouetta, was the same way, after suddenly losing her husband not long after they raised a family of six children and he retired. I never saw her wallow in a pity party. Instead, I witnessed her caring for her family and others around her in need. She remained strong in her faith, served joyfully in her church, traveled, and constantly focused on the blessings in her life. As a widow with deep faith, she rested in the assurance that Jesus already overcame death and made a way for us to spend eternity in heaven with Him. She knew her late husband would be there waiting when she arrived. Death, for all its wrenching pain, is not the end of the story in the life of a believer. Like Mary—and Jouetta—grieving was eventually tempered by the peace of what is to come.

Prayer: Loving God, please remind us of the beautiful lessons we see in the marriage of Mary and Joseph. For

those of us who are married, or hope to be, help us in the midst of all our challenges to find our way to an "us." Show us how to die to self and operate as a team committed to caring for and esteeming each other. Comfort us in our loneliness, and in those times when we are apart.

ESTHER AND XERXES

Marriage to a Monarch

The Book of Esther

Today's ideas about romance and love are far removed from what we see in the Bible. On the one hand, God's ideal design portrayed in the early chapters of Genesis is now deemed unrealistic and outdated by many. On the other hand, we see scores of examples in the Bible of flawed relationships God would never want us to emulate: concubines, sister wives, and women with little or no autonomy. That was often the norm in the ancient world, and it was wildly out of step with the loving partnership created for Adam and Eve in the Garden of Eden.

Marriage as set forth by God in Genesis calls for mutual surrender and radical union. The Bible is full of the stories of real men and women who—like us—stumbled in their efforts to live up to God's call. Abraham and Sarah, Isaac and Rebekah, Jacob and his wives—the Bible gives us plenty of examples of marriages where one partner (or both) struggled with selfishness, pride, manipulation, even betrayal. There is always something to be learned, no matter how disastrous the results. God is always working, even when we fall short. I find that deeply reassuring!

What I love about so many of the portrayals of women in the Bible is that God esteems them over and over again, despite their circumstances and messy relationships. He highlights their faithfulness, recognizes their sorrow, hears their cries, redeems them, and celebrates them. As we saw with the creation of Eve, from the beginning God was clear that women were valuable and essential partners to men, not simply accessories. In contrast to a modern world that often pits the genders against each other, the Bible gives us a vision of interdependent genders. We need each other.

That's all very important to remember in the midst of King Xerxes and Esther's story. It's not like a Western rom-com, though some have tried to reduce it to that. This isn't just a beauty pageant on steroids; it's God's divine work in the midst of a less-than-ideal marriage. Plenty of godly women find themselves in marriages with husbands who don't share their faith. There are plenty of ways to arrive there, but it doesn't mean God can't work through it. It's clear that a faithful woman can change the course of history, whether her spouse is a spiritual leader or not. God used Esther's devotion to her people—His people—to move the heart of a king with the earthly power to influence the course of history.

This all happened despite Xerxes' lack of awareness that God was working through him. As you'll quickly see, Xerxes was prideful and impulsive. It doesn't look like he placed much value on women as individuals, at least not when we first meet him. What is important is that his eventual wife, Esther, was faithful and discerning. She was sensitive and courageous. Throughout their story we see Xerxes' growing admiration and eventual joy in granting his wife's deepest wish in her greatest moment of need. These were two imperfect people, but God scripted their story and used what each brought to the table in order to accomplish His divine purposes.

It makes sense that when we read the book of Esther, we see the spotlight shining on her. I mean, she is the star of the show. But at the heart of the book is a marriage that came together in a way that probably would have been impossible for us to fathom in modern society—that is, until reality TV showed up on the scene. However it started, the union of Xerxes and Esther is full of wisdom and truth about how God can use marriage to His glory and for His purposes.

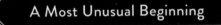

A Most Unusual Beginning

The first time we see Xerxes, he comes off as the epitome of a capricious, tyrannical monarch. In the first chapter of Esther, he sent away his wife Queen Vashti for a breach of royal protocol. But a little background first. After displaying all of his profound wealth for six months, Xerxes was hosting a blowout—a seven-day feast for anyone and everyone. The usual custom in the Persian court had been for all of the kings' subjects to drink when he drank. Imagine: instead of having a good time at the party, constantly watching the king to see whether or not you should be taking a sip. Doesn't sound like much fun! But Xerxes had actually reversed this custom so that "each guest was allowed to drink with no restrictions." (Esther 1:8) That sounds like the act of a somewhat generous person who wanted people to relax and enjoy themselves. But the Hebrew word translated in that verse as "guest" is a masculine word. These guys were having a good time, while Vashti had her own royal feast underway for the women of the palace.

So, Xerxes had been showing off for months and he was coming to the close of seven days of eating and drinking around the clock. Esther 1:10 tells us the king "was in high spirits from wine" when he demanded that Queen Vashti be brought in. Xerxes wanted her to come wearing her royal crown, "in order to display her beauty to the people and nobles, for she was lovely to look at." (Esther 1:11) He'd been flaunting all the treasures of his kingdom, and to Xerxes that's what Vashti was—just another one of his pretty possessions that could be used to impress others. Only, she decided she wasn't going to do it. Based on the customs and restrictions of that time, I'm stunned—and the king was too! In fact, he was royally ticked. We're told he "became furious and burned with anger." (Esther 1:12)

You can see how this isn't going to end well for Vashti. She had no real power, and her refusal to obey the king's order would be viewed as the most egregious, disrespectful thing she could have done. And to do it in front of all the men? What a slap in the face to Xerxes. Of course he was livid. As king, Xerxes likely could have done anything he chose in this scenario, but he leaned on "wise" men in his court to help him craft an appropriate response—and they didn't hold back. This public refusal to obey the king would have ramifications far beyond Vashti. One of the nobles advised the king:

> This very day the Persian and Median women of the nobility who have heard about the queen's conduct will re-

spond to all the king's nobles in the same way. There will be no end of disrespect and discord.

Therefore, if it pleases the king, let him issue a royal decree and let it be written in the laws of Persia and Media, which cannot be repealed, that Vashti is never again to enter the presence of King Xerxes. Also let the king give her royal position to someone else who is better than she. Then when the king's edict is proclaimed throughout all his vast realm, all the women will respect their husbands, from the least to the greatest.

Esther 1:18–20

There's more than a touch of insecure panic in their representation of the chaos that will supposedly result from Vashti's disobedience. *Listen up, Xerxes, she embarrassed you and now we're gonna have the same situation on our hands if you don't make an example out of her—stat!* They both appealed to Xerxes' pride *and* selfishly sought to make sure they didn't end up in the same dilemma. The Queen was banished.

All of this paranoia, anger, and distrust didn't bode well for his next wife. And how Xerxes went about getting that new queen was far from an attempt to find an intellectual match or equal partner: he held a kind of kingdom-wide bridal competition. That may sound intriguing, but the more we learn about the contest it starts to sound like the worst reality TV show ever conceived (and that's saying something)! It's highly unlikely the women of Persia had much of a say about getting caught up in this game, including Esther. The king's advisers—yes, those guys again—had a plan.

> Let the king appoint commissioners in every province of his realm to bring all these beautiful young women into the harem at the citadel of Susa. Let them be placed under the care of Hegai, the king's eunuch, who is in charge of the women; and let beauty treatments be given to them.
>
> Esther 2:3

Okay, so government officials were sent out all over the kingdom to find hot women to be taken to the palace and join the harem and be put through makeovers. Then the king would take his pick. Got it.

Esther is described as "having a lovely figure and beautiful," (Esther 2:7) so you better believe she was among those *taken* to the palace (v. 8). An orphan, she had been raised by her cousin Mordecai. He cautioned her not to reveal her Jewish ancestry and family background when she got there. Immediately we see that she was highly favored by Hegai, who gave her the best treatments, several attendants, and a plum living space. Mordecai could only watch from a distance but walked by the court where she was living to try to find out how she was doing. The Bible makes clear she was flourishing. Verse 15 tells us, "Esther won the favor of everyone who saw her." But the only one who truly mattered was Xerxes, and he was definitely mesmerized as well.

> Now the king was attracted to Esther more than to any of the other women, and she won his favor and approval more than any of the other virgins. So he set a royal crown on her head and made her queen instead of Vashti. And

the king gave a great banquet, Esther's banquet, for all his nobles and officials. He proclaimed a holiday throughout the provinces and distributed gifts with royal liberality.

Esther 2:17–18

Well, that was quick! No time for a final question from the judges or naming any runners-up. Xerxes liked what he saw. The King James Version says he "loved" her. Whatever the connection, he had found his winner and the orphaned Jewish girl was now the Queen of Persia.

Esther won the prize, but did it feel like any kind of victory to her? At no point did Xerxes (or anyone else) ask her what her opinion was about any of this, or consider what she might want. While it's probably no surprise after the way he treated Vashti, Xerxes' entitled behavior likely made Esther feel powerless and anxious. She would always know her entire future was dependent on his impressions of her and staying on his good side. As with Queen Vashti, Queen Esther was just one more possession to be displayed at a banquet, one more lovely ornament for the royal court. What a way to begin a relationship!

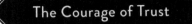

The Courage of Trust

The book of Esther is the story of a young woman finding her courage, and of God using a pagan king to save His people. The Lord can work His will and His way through leaders whether they acknowledge or serve him—or not!

> In the LORD's hand the king's heart is a stream of water
> that he channels toward all who please him.
> Proverbs 21:1

> He changes times and seasons;
> he deposes kings and raises up others.
> He gives wisdom to the wise
> and knowledge to the discerning.
> Daniel 2:21

God's ability to get things done is never dependent on an earthly leader, and they're also no hindrance to His plans. While Xerxes may not have had a soft spot for the Jewish people or their God, he certainly had one for his new Queen—a woman perfectly positioned "for such a time as this." (Esther 4:14)

Esther was lodged in luxury and comfort in the palace, but it must have been a lonely and alienating experience for her in some ways. A young Jewish woman whose birth name was Hadassah, Esther could never have expected to find herself raised to the highest echelons of power in the Persian Empire. As reflected in her use of a Persian name, Esther was used to blending in, but the stakes had never before been this high. Everything depended on her performing according to the customs of the Persian culture in which she lived, winning favor among the backstabbing courtiers in the palace. She could not afford to be openly Jewish around her Persian neighbors, including her own husband.

She trusted in the wisdom and guidance of Mordecai, who was about to make a brave move of his own. With Esther tucked away in the palace, Mordecai stayed as close as possible. It was when he was sitting at the king's gate that he heard two of the king's own men angry and conspiring to kill him. Mordecai was able to feed that information to the Queen, who told Xerxes and gave Mordecai all the credit. The two men were executed and the whole thing was tucked away in the king's record books, only for the good deed to be rediscovered by the king much later.

With those two men gone, Xerxes elevated Haman to serve above all the other princes and nobles. Haman was a descendant of the man who was once king of one of Israel's fiercest foes: the Amalekites. So while everyone else groveled at his feet, Mordecai refused, and that infuriated Haman. That fury was the genesis of Haman's plot to wipe out the Jewish people within the reach of the Persian Empire. Haman went to the king with a carefully scripted case against the Jewish people, and walked out with the right to craft a royal decree calling for their annihilation. Haman didn't want to simply punish Mordecai, he wanted to destroy the Jews. And thanks to God's divine design, one of them had already captured the king's heart.

We don't know much about how Esther and Xerxes' relationship progressed, but she would remain in a subservient position. She would go to him when summoned, but otherwise hang around the palace awaiting that call. To go to him unbidden was unthinkable and illegal, and could cost Esther her life. So it's understandable that when Mordecai got word of Haman's murderous plot to Esther, she at first hesitated to go to Xerxes.

All the king's officials and the people of the royal provinces know that for any man or woman who approaches the king in the inner court without being summoned the king has but one law: that they be put to death unless the king extends the gold scepter to them and spares their lives. But thirty days have passed since I was called to go to the king.

Esther 4:11

Mordecai knew the risk, but he didn't mince words.

Do not think that because you are in the king's house you alone of all the Jews will escape. For if you remain silent at this time, relief and deliverance for the Jews will arise from another place, but you and your father's family will perish. And who knows but that you have come to your royal position for such a time as this?

Esther 4:13b–14

That's when Esther asked all the Jews to join her in fasting for three days, as she prepared to go to the king—knowing it could end in her execution.

Let's stop a minute here to consider how odd this relationship was. Esther was Queen by none of her own doing. She was taken to the king and entered into his warped contest, where her charm and beauty won everyone over. Xerxes was crazy about Esther on some level, but they did not have the kind of marriage we cherish and expect today—with love, respect, and partnership. Yet we never see Esther bristle against her role or try to escape it. She faithfully follows Mordecai's sage advice and carries out her duties. We have no way of knowing whether or not she'd fallen in love with the king at this point.

Against this backdrop, Esther summoned the courage to appear before the king—to take the initiative. This was an offense as grave as Queen Vashti's. The prior queen had been stripped of her title because she had mistakenly believed that she was in charge of her own comings and goings, not the king. Esther's bold move to approach the king could been seen as the same kind of disrespectful show of independence. But there was a difference; Esther was risking not just the divorce and banishment that Vashti had earned: she was risking death. Esther wasn't disobeying a summons; she was inventing her own summons. All the more worrying because, last time, Xerxes had been guided by his advisers, and Esther's whole mission was to attack Xerxes' new second-in-command: Haman.

But she still did it. Esther put on her royal robes and stood in the king's hall, waiting for a chance to appear before her husband. The Bible tells us that "when he saw Queen Esther standing in the court, he was pleased with her and held out to her the gold scepter that was in his hand." (Esther 5:2) Rather than an instant execution, or even a rebuke, it seems the king was happy to see Esther. No doubt, God had seen the fasting and preparation of his people—supporting Esther as she put her life on the line for all of theirs.

For Esther to have appeared before the king without invitation showed a great deal of trust that she would be spared. We know—because at this point we know far more about Esther than her husband does—that the source of her trust was in God and God's care for her people. But Xerxes didn't. Maybe he thought Esther's appearance was an act of trust in *him*. She was appealing to his love and his mercy. This time, he didn't pause to speak with his advisers. He responded to her immediately, and we see our first glimpse of an actual conversation between husband and wife:

Then the king asked, "What is it, Queen Esther? What is your request? Even up to half the kingdom, it will be given you."

"If it pleases the king," replied Esther, "let the king, together with Haman, come today to a banquet I have prepared for him."

Esther 5:3–4

The phrase "If it pleases the king" reminds me of one of the very first things I learned in law school. We'd engage in mock courtroom scenarios and it was drilled into our brains that the first thing you always say when addressing the judge—or judges—before beginning your argument is, "May it please the court?" It signals complete deference to the person—or people—who will decide the fate of your client. Esther was wise in her diplomacy to the king. Having escaped immediate banishment or death, she continued to diplomatically appeal to the one man who could throw out a death sentence for millions.

It worked like a charm.

"Bring Haman at once," the king said, "so that we may do what Esther asks."

Esther 5:3–5a

This was not a king irritated or upset with his daring queen, not by a long shot. He wanted to grant his wife what she wanted—even up to half of his kingdom. It's nearly unimaginable that a modest, orphaned Jewish woman would be given half of the Persian Empire. Did the king mean it or was he simply trying to impress his queen? Either way, Esther had found favor with a man who had no idea exactly whom he was married to!

This was an extraordinary and phenomenal show of faith in Esther. It wasn't just a show of faith; it was an exaltation. Xerxes offered half of all his kingdom to his wife, which would arguably make her his equal! At this point it sure seems as though Xerxes was more than just "attracted to" or "pleased with" Esther. This extravagant offer was the gesture of a man who very much wanted to reassure Esther that she was safe and esteemed, but also a man who wanted her to think well of *him*. We have gone from a king who believed a woman was his possession to a king offering to surrender his most prized possessions to a woman he valued.

What an interesting reversal of the Xerxes we saw at the beginning of the story, when he insisted that Vashti hurry to do as he commanded. We find him doing just the opposite for Esther, acting as her benefactor trying to fulfill her request as quickly as possible.

What could account for this change in Xerxes' attitude? Was it genuine love? We have to be careful when we talk about romantic love in the context of the Bible. So much of the "hearts and flowers" culture of romance that seems natural to us today would have seemed very strange to the people of the ancient world. But we shouldn't assume that means there was no romance in the Bible at all. Remember Jacob's love-at-first-sight glimpse of Rachel? How about Isaac falling for Rebekah? We can't know what was at the core of Xerxes' attraction to Esther over time, but we know he acted like a changed man in her presence.

Once they got to that banquet, Xerxes must have grown

confused with his beautiful wife. I've often imagined how Esther must have felt, knowing what was at stake. Was her heart thumping in her chest as she tried to find the right time—and the perfect words—to accuse the king's most favored adviser?

> As they were drinking wine, the king again asked Esther, "Now what is your petition? It will be given you. And what is your request? Even up to half the kingdom, it will be granted."
>
> Esther replied, "My petition and my request is this: If the king regards me with favor and if it pleases the king to grant my petition and fulfill my request, let the king and Haman come tomorrow to the banquet I will prepare for them. Then I will answer the king's question."
>
> Esther 5:6–8

Esther, who had spent her whole existence as queen carefully avoiding displeasing the king, still played for time. She deferred to the next night, and asked the king and Haman to come again, for another dinner party. Esther knew what a big bombshell she was going to drop.

She would ask her husband to believe that Haman could be cruel enough to plan the genocide of thousands of people. She would ask the king to choose her over Haman. Did she hesitate in order to see if Xerxes was willing to put himself at her disposal for another night? How far would he extend his goodwill? Could she trust him?

By the way, Haman left that first banquet so high on himself that when he encountered Mordecai—who once again refused to bow to him or show any fear—he went home and came up with a plot to ask the king's permission to kill him. Haman bragged about how much the king trusted him and how Esther kept inviting him to these exclusive banquets, then added this:

> But all this gives me no satisfaction as long as I see that Jew Mordecai sitting at the king's gate.
> Esther 5:13

So arrogant and self-absorbed with wiping out the one person who wouldn't bow to him, Haman couldn't even enjoy the lavish life of prestige he was living. It would lead to his downfall, as God worked through Esther and her marriage to a pagan king.

Protection and Loyalty

In the third encounter we see between Xerxes and Esther, the Queen finally told her husband the truth. But in between the first dinner party and the second, something happened that may show us a bit of Xerxes' evolution as a man and as a leader. When the king was reminded that Mordecai had once been instrumental in saving him from an assassination attempt, yet had never received the reward he deserved for his heroism, Xerxes decided to set things right. Xerxes decreed (ironically, at the suggestion of Haman, who believed these honors were being prepared for him) that Mordecai should be paraded through the city on a royal horse and attired in fine robes, with heralds to go before him commanding people to honor him.

At that point, the king had no clue about the close family relationship between his queen and Mordecai. The man had spoken up to rescue the king long before and never grumbled or asked why the king hadn't honored him. Xerxes wasn't looking to impress Mordecai or win him over. The Bible tells us simply that the king took "delight" in looking for a way to honor the man who had saved his life (Esther 6:6). Had Xerxes matured to the point of being motivated by gratefulness and integrity rather than impulse and ego? Esther was about to find out just where her husband stood.

At their second banquet with Haman, the king again reassured his queen that he wanted to grant her deepest wishes—again offering up to half his kingdom. He'd slept on it, and the deal was still on the table. But Esther wanted nothing of his riches, she needed something much more valuable: the power of his royal decree. What courage it took to accuse the king's right-hand man and expose her true identity.

"If I have found favor with you, Your Majesty, and if it pleases you, grant me my life—this is my petition. And spare my people—this is my request. For I and my people have been sold to be destroyed, killed and annihilated. If we had merely been sold as male and female slaves, I would have kept quiet, because no such distress would justify disturbing the king." King Xerxes asked Queen Esther, "Who is he? Where is he—the man who has dared to do such a thing?" Esther said, "An adversary and enemy! This vile Haman!" Then Haman was terrified before the king and queen. The king got up in a rage, left his wine and went out into the palace garden. But Haman, realizing that the king had already decided his fate, stayed behind to beg Queen Esther for his life.

Esther 7:3–7

Even in this life-or-death request, Esther wisely offered humility. *If we were only going to be enslaved, I would never have dared to bother you.* And then she delivered the gut punch: it's Haman. The king, her husband, was so furious at this threat to his wife that he stormed out. Haman knew it was curtains for him.

In his attempt to spare his own life, Haman made one last fatal move.

Just as the king returned from the palace garden to the banquet hall, Haman was falling on the couch where Esther was reclining. The king exclaimed, "Will he even molest the queen while she is with me in the house?" As soon as the word left the king's mouth, they covered Haman's face. Then Harbona, one of the eunuchs attending the king, said, "A pole reaching to a height of fifty cubits stands by Haman's house. He had it set up for Mordecai, who spoke up to help the king." The king said, "Impale him on it!" So they impaled Haman on the pole he had set up for Mordecai. Then the king's fury subsided.

Esther 7: 8–10

Esther's trust in her royal husband was well-placed; he didn't let her down. Xerxes never questioned whether she was telling the truth, and there was no hesitation on his part. An attack on the king's wife was an attack on him and was treated accordingly as a treasonous act, deserving of all the king's fury.

A New Family

Now it was time for King Xerxes to get the rest of the story. The very same day Haman was executed, Esther told the king the truth about Mordecai and introduced the two. The man who had once saved the king's life was actually related to him by marriage!

> That same day King Xerxes gave Queen Esther the estate of Haman, the enemy of the Jews. And Mordecai came into the presence of the king, for Esther had told how he was related to her. The king took off his signet ring, which he had reclaimed from Haman, and presented it to Mordecai. And Esther appointed him over Haman's estate.
> Esther 8:1–2

In the end, of course, it wasn't Haman's worldly treasures that Esther wanted, but a revocation of the decree calling for the murder of all the Jews of the Persian Empire. But there was a major problem: "No document written in the king's name and sealed with his ring can be revoked." (Esther 8:8) That meant the death sentence for the Jewish people couldn't simply be thrown out.

Esther once again showed humility when she went to her husband on behalf of her people, just as God had positioned her to do.

"If it pleases the king," she said, "and if he regards me with favor and thinks it the right thing to do, and if he is pleased with me, let an order be written overruling the dispatches that Haman son of Hammedatha, the Agagite, devised and wrote to destroy the Jews in all the king's provinces. For how can I bear to see disaster fall on my people? How can I bear to see the destruction of my family?"

Esther 8:5–6

Not only did the king grant his wife's request, he gave Esther and Mordecai the authority to write the very wording of the new decree and the right to seal it with the king's ring—which had been entrusted to Mordecai.

The new decree, which gave the Jewish people the right to assemble and defend themselves, was quickly written in multiple languages and sent to the farthest reaches of the Empire on lightning-fast horses bred just for the king. The document also gave the Jews the right "to plunder the property of their enemies." (Esther 8:11) The Bible tells us what happened next. There was great joy and feasting and "many people of other nationalities became Jews." (Esther 8:17)

The Xerxes we meet at the end of the book of Esther stands in enormous contrast to the impetuous, haughty man we first encountered. We can't know exactly what happened in his head or in his heart, but we know he had enormous respect for Esther and Mordecai. She had no choice about how she entered Xerxes' world, but she remained faithful to the advice of Mordecai and summoned the courage to graciously and bravely fight for her people.

Xerxes became a defender of the Jewish people. Not only had

he gained a wife of great honor, but Mordecai had also proven to be a devoted subject of outstanding character. While Esther was undoubtedly deeply grateful for Xerxes' unwavering protection and devotion to her cause, we never find out if she truly fell in love with him. As often as their story is portrayed as a fairytale romance, what this marriage brought about is something much different—and much more important.

Bottom line: our relationship—or spouse—doesn't have to be perfect in order for God to work through it. Esther and Xerxes' relationship is probably one we can't relate to at all! But what a beautiful picture it paints of what God can do when we are humble and surrender to His will, even in the midst of unusual circumstances.

Prayer: Heavenly Father, please help us to see that You are always working through our circumstances and our lives—even when our situations are less than the ideal we hope and pray for. May we find the courage to speak up in the moments we find ourselves in the midst of a difficult assignment. Give us the discernment to make our case with wisdom and humility and to trust You with the outcome.

RUTH AND BOAZ

Second Chances

The Book of Ruth

There are moments in life when the unthinkable happens, leaving us reeling. In the wake of a tragedy our human nature will often spark endless questions. *How will I ever recover from this? How will I survive? Why would God ever allow this? What good will ever come from this nightmare?* For nearly three years of a worldwide pandemic many of us have asked these questions over and over. Our family lost people we loved, as did so many of you reading these words. Hearts were broken. Dreams died. In the fog of those dark days, we often looked around and thought life would never be easy again. There didn't seem to be many exits from the valleys of loss and upheaval. Some of you may still be there, and it's my prayer this story of Ruth and Boaz will offer you a heavy dose of hope.

The story of Ruth and Boaz has the makings of a blockbuster movie: heartbreak, struggle, faith, hope, and redemption. Throw in a couple of unexpected plot twists and you're left with a beautiful example of God's masterful planning. He is the God of second chances not only in our spiritual lives, but in our earthly ones as well. Ruth and Boaz's story wasn't the common match we often see in ancient communities portrayed in the Bible. They weren't a young couple born of an arranged marriage designed to benefit their families. Instead, God was their ultimate Matchmaker, bringing them together after deep grief and loss. We all know someone who's suffered the loss of a spouse—whether through widowhood or divorce. Maybe you're walking through that challenge right now. That's right where we first meet Ruth.

Ruth's story takes up the whole first chapter of the book. Ruth was from Moab, an ancient kingdom just across the Dead Sea from the land of Israel, where modern Jordan is today. She had married a young man from Israel who had emigrated to Moab during a famine along with his parents and his brother. Some period of time before their marriage, Ruth's father-in-law, Elimelek, had died. That left her mother-in-law, Naomi, widowed but still with two sons to carry on the family name and watch over her. Naomi's other son had married a woman named Orpah. Sadly, Naomi lost both her sons. That left a trio of women with no protectors or providers. I have written in *Women of the Bible Speak* and *Mothers and Daughters of the Bible Speak* about the complete devastation the men's deaths meant for these women. They would have been left extremely vulnerable both physically and financially.

It was against that backdrop that Naomi got a little bit of good news, in that conditions in her homeland had improved. She decided to return to Bethlehem and urged her daughters-in-law to start their lives over with new husbands and families. Naomi was a deeply heartbroken person by this time. She fled the land of her birth because of famine, an affliction that was often seen as a sign of God's judgment. In all her loss, Naomi had begun to believe God Himself was working against her. She told her daughters-in-law, "It is exceedingly bitter to me for your sake that the hand of the Lord has gone out against me." (Ruth 2:13b) When Naomi finally arrived in Bethlehem, she told her old acquaintances that God had allowed tragedy and misfortune to scar her life (Ruth 1:20).

It wouldn't be until much later that Naomi would realize God had never abandoned her, but in the midst of her devastation it must have felt that way. Have you walked that road? Have there been times when you felt God had abandoned you? I firmly believe that God understands our questioning and lamenting. Emotions are not sinful, they're God-given. We can find ourselves in very dark, discouraging places. Sometimes it's our own doing, but often we experience anguish through no fault of our own.

I'm reminded of the desperate father in Mark 9. Jesus' ministry had become public, and there were often crowds following Him and begging for miracles. The man brought his son who was suffering greatly because he was possessed. See his desperate cry for help.

"But if you can do anything, take pity on us and help us."

"'If you can'?" said Jesus. "Everything is possible for one who believes."

Immediately the boy's father exclaimed, "I do believe; help me overcome my unbelief!"

Mark 9:22b–24

I've prayed this countless times myself. *Lord, I don't know what you're doing in this situation, and I'm in a lot of pain. Please help me to believe where the doubts are creeping in!* God hears and answers those prayers.

Despite her hopelessness Naomi's faith must have been strong because even though she tried to turn away her daughter-in-law, Ruth insisted on traveling with her and fully embracing everything about her mother-in-law's life. Ruth's stirring words of commitment are often repeated today. She pledged to stay where Naomi stayed, to make Naomi's people her people, and—most important—to make Naomi's God her God (Ruth 1:16). Ruth embraced Naomi's faith, and God would honor that in countless ways.

Ruth's words of sacrifice and commitment still move us today, often as part of marriage ceremonies. Imagine how much more powerful they must have been to an ancient reader. After all, this woman was a Moabite—not just a foreigner, but someone far removed from the covenant God had made with Israel. Moabites were actually traditional enemies of Israel. So for Ruth to have made these vows to her mother-in-law was truly extraordinary. She felt deep love for her mother-in-law and an abiding sense of duty to serve and protect her. Perhaps Ruth also believed there would be a chance at a new life for her in Bethlehem too, a chance for God to redeem her pain and suffering.

By turning her back on the security of her home in Moab and choosing poverty with her mother-in-law, we see not only Ruth's courage but also her kindness. Courage and kindness—two traits we don't often see united in the Bible or indeed in our own lives. When we think of the courage of a warrior, we don't tend to think at the same time of kindness and gentleness. We see both in Ruth, and Boaz would too. But we're not there just yet!

The First Encounter

We catch a glimpse of Boaz not long before Ruth does.

> **Now Naomi had a relative on her husband's side, a man of standing from the clan of Elimelek, whose name was Boaz.**
>   Ruth 2:1

Boaz is described only as "a man of standing." We learn in short order that he owned several fields, and employed harvesters and overseers. In other words, he was likely wealthy. But the word used to describe him in Ruth 2:1 means more than just well-off, which is why a lot of English translations use phrases like "a man of standing," or "a man of substance." He is described as an *ish gibor hayil*—literally, a mighty and valorous man. *Hayil* is often used to describe warriors and people or animals who are exceptionally strong and courageous—lions, hunters, soldiers, leaders.

Boaz was "valorous" in his community in the sense that he was important or powerful, but also lurking behind that word was the idea of a warrior's capability and courage. This is important to note because it shows us a common link of courage between Boaz and Ruth, and tells us that these two people shared some significant character traits. In fact, later in the story, Boaz would use the exact same Hebrew word to describe Ruth! (Ruth 3:11)

We see in Boaz's life the way duty and joy can intertwine. He scrupulously followed the law of Moses, not simply with his words but with his actions. He gave a religious greeting to his workers and followed it up by taking care to leave the gleanings of his harvest for the poor and the sojourner. Boaz had been blessed by God. He lived in a land of no famine, and had great wealth. He saw in that not an invitation to make all of life a party, but to bless those around him. It was his duty, but it also resulted in great joy. He was literally carrying forward God's command to Abraham, to take his chosen status and use it to be a blessing to the nations (Genesis 12:1-3).

The scene has been set for Ruth and Boaz to meet for the first time:

> And Ruth the Moabite said to Naomi, "Let me go to the fields and pick up the leftover grain behind anyone in whose eyes I find favor." Naomi said to her, "Go ahead, my daughter." So she went out, entered a field and began to glean behind the harvesters. As it turned out, she was working in a field belonging to Boaz, who was from the clan of Elimelek.
> Ruth 2:2-3

Let's pause here for just a moment on the phrase "As it turned out." In Hebrew the wording is actually "her chance chanced." Huh! What a coincidence that faithful, humble, hard-working Ruth just so happened to wind up in Boaz's field. God is always working, even when we are unaware.

There have been some amazing occurrences in my life that can't be explained by anything other than God's providence. Years ago, I was trying to make a business decision that required me to choose between two selections. I'd narrowed the choice down to two people who seemed like excellent options—one man and one woman. Both were exceptionally qualified and connected and could help me get something accomplished that I was working on. As always, Sheldon and I prayed that God would guide us to the right path. Around that same time, I was going through some old books ("My name is Shannon and I am a book hoarder") and trying to get things in order. I have several different versions of the Bible, and I picked up one I hadn't used in my studies for a while. Inside was tucked a piece of paper with a name and address on it—from a meeting ten years earlier. It was the very woman I was talking to about the new business venture I was working on. I'm convinced the Lord pointed me back to the memory of that meeting years before when both she and I were much less experienced and trying to find our way professionally. Because of the discovery of that note tucked away in an old Bible, we've now worked together for years, both of us accomplishing things professionally we couldn't have imagined!

That tattered piece of paper wasn't a coincidence, and neither was Ruth's decision to work in a field that belonged to Boaz.

Just then Boaz arrived from Bethlehem and greeted the harvesters, "The LORD be with you!"

"The LORD bless you!" they answered. Boaz asked the overseer of his harvesters, "Who does that young woman belong to?" The overseer replied, "She is the Moabite who came back from Moab with Naomi. She said, 'Please let me glean and gather among the sheaves behind the harvesters.' She came into the field and has remained here from morning till now, except for a short rest in the shelter."

Ruth 2:4–7

Desperate for food and support, Ruth had gone out into the fields to do what the poorest of the poor did—pick up grain that the harvesters had dropped and use whatever she could collect to make bread for herself and Naomi.

The very first thing Boaz did when he showed up at the fields was to invoke the name of the Lord, the God whom Ruth had sworn would be her own. What happened next was the first conversation between Boaz and Ruth. It is full of kindness and generosity. What a beautiful place for a love story to begin.

> So Boaz said to Ruth, "My daughter, listen to me. Don't go and glean in another field and don't go away from here. Stay here with the women who work for me. Watch the field where the men are harvesting, and follow along after the women. I have told the men not to lay a hand on you. And whenever you are thirsty, go and get a drink from the water jars the men have filled."
> Ruth 2:8–9

What a radical change from the circumstances Naomi and Ruth found themselves in when they arrived in Bethlehem. Ruth's humility led her to get to work, knowing and accepting the gravity of her and Naomi's situation. And that hadn't gone unnoticed.

When Ruth reacted with great surprise and gratitude, we find out Boaz knew quite a bit more about her than she likely imagined.

> Boaz replied, "I've been told all about what you have done for your mother-in-law since the death of your husband—

how you left your father and mother and your homeland
and came to live with a people you did not know before.
May the LORD repay you for what you have done. May you
be richly rewarded by the LORD, the God of Israel, under
whose wings you have come to take refuge."
    Ruth 2:11–12

This widow who had suffered crushing loss was about to get
the second chance she'd probably never dared to imagine, and
it all turned on the fact that she had decided to dedicate herself
both to serving someone else in need and committing to God's
ways.

Boaz had heard about Ruth long before they had met. He was
clearly moved by what she had done, and knew all the details. It's
possible that not everything he had heard had been flattering,
either. The ancient world was a highly insular society, and few
were very fond of foreigners. There were probably grumblings
and gossip about the Moabite woman Naomi had brought back
with her. But Boaz saw only a woman of extraordinary courage
and kindness, and he also knew about Ruth's conversion to the
God of Israel.

Ruth responded to his compassion by telling Boaz that even
the way he spoke to his servants had put her "at ease" (Ruth 2:13b),
quickly adding that she didn't consider herself to even have the
standing of one of them. Was that a clue that maybe not everyone
had been as kind to the outsider as Boaz was? He didn't see Ruth
as simply a foreigner. He saw a fellow believer in God, and treated
her accordingly. By giving Ruth servant status in his field, he had
already acted with extraordinary generosity. But Boaz was about
to do more:

At mealtime Boaz said to her, "Come over here. Have some bread and dip it in the wine vinegar." When she sat down with the harvesters, he offered her some roasted grain. She ate all she wanted and had some left over. As she got up to glean, Boaz gave orders to his men, "Let her gather among the sheaves and don't reprimand her. Even pull out some stalks for her from the bundles and leave them for her to pick up, and don't rebuke her." So Ruth gleaned in the field until evening. Then she threshed the barley she had gathered, and it amounted to about an ephah.

Ruth 2:14–17

I don't know why, but this always makes me feel teary-eyed when I read it. Ruth was in such difficult circumstances: a young widow and an outsider working the fields to survive. Boaz made sure she not only had her immediate needs met, but he also cooked up a plan to make sure her hard work would provide even more benefit than she could expect.

Ruth was overjoyed to return to Naomi with an abundance of harvest and to explain the good fortune she'd experienced. Naomi celebrated the good news with her daughter-in-law, who then revealed it was a man named Boaz who had shown her such kindness. "The Lord bless him!" Naomi exclaimed, then added:

That man is our close relative; he is one of our guardian-redeemers.

Ruth 2:20b

The phrase *kinsman-redeemer* is also used in this context. It means a male relative with the legal responsibility to help a family member in financial distress (Leviticus 25:25). Again, it was no coincidence that God had led Ruth to Boaz's field—and to his protection.

The Second Encounter

Ruth stayed with the harvesters "until the barley and wheat harvests were finished," likely giving Boaz even more time to get to know her—or at least to see her continued hard work. As Naomi began to think of what should come next for Ruth, she raised the possibility of a match with Boaz. Naomi guided Ruth in how to properly approach him about the chance he would want to take legal responsibility for her.

> "Tonight he will be winnowing barley on the threshing floor. Wash, put on perfume, and get dressed in your best clothes. Then go down to the threshing floor, but don't let him know you are there until he has finished eating and drinking. When he lies down, note the place where he is lying. Then go and uncover his feet and lie down. He will tell you what to do."
>
> "I will do whatever you say," Ruth answered. So she went down to the threshing floor and did everything her mother-in-law told her to do.
>
> Ruth 3:2b–6

Naomi hoped Boaz would fulfill his role of guardian-redeemer for the two of them by marrying Ruth. As a Moabite, the plan may have seemed strange to Ruth. In ancient Israel, there was no social safety net, and families were expected to provide for their own. If there were widows or vulnerable members of an extended family, the closest male relative was expected to care for them—to be their *goel*, their redeemer from harm. This principle was so powerful and important that God Himself is referred to as the *goel* of the people of Israel: "my Rock and my Redeemer," He is called in the words of Psalm 19:14.

There was no guarantee Boaz would say yes to taking on the burden of two penniless women with no other means of support. In fact, it was more likely he would decline. The usual way a *goel* would redeem a young unmarried woman was to marry her. A man couldn't take an unmarried woman into his house without causing a scandal, so marriage would have been the proper course. Ruth's case was complicated. For one thing, she was a foreigner. Plenty of men of Israel would have flinched at marrying a Moabite woman. Even worse, Ruth was a widow. The reality was that if she remarried and had a child under the concept of a levirate marriage, they would be considered descendants of her first husband. That was a way of preserving the family name and rights. But there was no denying this meant that there wasn't exactly a line forming around the block to marry a widow. In Ruth's case, a new husband would also take on an aging, widowed mother-in-law. Ruth had no reason to think that Boaz was going to say yes, and she went to him at night when no one else would be around. If he said no, she was spared the humiliation of a public refusal.

Boaz also was given the deference to make a private decision, one of great importance to everyone involved.

When Boaz had finished eating and drinking and was in good spirits, he went over to lie down at the far end of the grain pile. Ruth approached quietly, uncovered his feet and lay down. In the middle of the night something startled the man; he turned—and there was a woman lying at his feet! "Who are you?" he asked.

"I am your servant Ruth," she said. "Spread the corner of your garment over me, since you are a guardian-redeemer of our family."

"The LORD bless you, my daughter," he replied. "This kindness is greater than that which you showed earlier: You have not run after the younger men, whether rich or poor. And now, my daughter, don't be afraid. I will do for you all you ask. All the people of my town know that you are a woman of noble character."

Ruth 3:7-11

Boaz agreed to step up and help Ruth, but let's take note of the way he did it. Did he say, *Well, okay, I guess this is what I'm supposed to do, and I am a really generous guy?* No, nothing he said sounded like pity or charity.

God's law, in fact, makes it very clear that "charity" is not what we're supposed to give those in need. The Hebrew word for justice—*tzedek*—is the root of the word for charity, *tzedakah*. Giving to those in need is not simply an act of charity, but an act of righteousness or justice. It is what we are commanded to do; it is what the poor are owed. Jesus Himself made this point when He told his disciples, "So you also, when you have done everything you were told to do, should say, 'We are unworthy servants; we have only done our duty.'" (Luke 17:10) The Scripture of both Old and New Testaments is very clear: Our duty is to care for the poor.

Far from making Ruth feel like she should be grateful, Boaz expressed gratitude to her. He thanked her for being interested in him! He made the kind assumption that *she* was the one with something to give to *him*. He called her a young woman of noble character. He did everything he could to build her up, and to buoy her sense of self-worth. He must have known how much bravery it took to literally grovel at someone's feet and ask for their help. Boaz was quick to erase any humiliation Ruth may have felt.

If you and I are paying attention at this point, we can clearly see that Ruth and Boaz were both incredibly kind and responsive to the needs of others over and above what society expected of them. Ruth did not need to act with such extravagant commitment to Naomi, any more than Boaz needed to lavish generosity on Ruth. Ruth seemed caught off guard a bit at Boaz's unrestrained benevolence. In the wake of her own compassionate actions, was she pleasantly surprised that she could also be on the receiving end of unmerited graciousness?

Ruth and Boaz's story didn't start with a love-at-first-sight, thunderbolt-and-lightning kind of moment. It unfolded more slowly. Unlike just about any other love story in the Bible, this was a getting-to-know-you story. These two people were moved by the character and integrity they saw in each other. They each acted in honorable ways. They could have made very different—very selfish—decisions, and yet both Ruth and Boaz put others first and honored their God.

We also see further examples of Boaz's protection of Ruth in

what happened that night. Though he revealed there was another, closer guardian-redeemer who had the right of first refusal
to Ruth's hand in marriage, Boaz urged her to stay under his protection until morning. He also saw to it that no one would know
she had been there overnight. Finally, he sent her away with a
generous gift of barley she could easily use to provide for herself and Naomi. Ruth's mother-in-law was happy to hear how the
overture had been received, and assured her that Boaz would
quickly see about the other man who had a right to step into the
situation on Ruth's behalf.

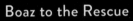

Boaz to the Rescue

Ruth is so important that often when we tell her story, we think
of the whole narrative from Ruth's point of view. In fact, the story
is much more balanced than that, and in the last chapter (Ruth 4)
we see Boaz acting alone, apart from Ruth. He did exactly what
he told her he would—and more. He went to sit at the gate of Bethlehem, where important men of the city met to transact business.
After taking his place among the city leaders, he approached
Naomi's other relative, whose right to be *goel* was equal to or
better than his own. Boaz wanted to make sure that no one had
cause for complaint against him, or against Ruth.

Boaz first presented the fact that Naomi was selling a piece of
land that had belonged to her late husband. He offered the other
potential guardian-redeemer the opportunity to rightfully pur-
chase it in front of all the elders. The man quickly replied that he

would do so. Boaz then revealed that the entire deal would also involve taking on Ruth the widow. Time out.

> At this, the guardian-redeemer said, "Then I cannot redeem it because I might endanger my own estate. You redeem it yourself. I cannot do it."
> Ruth 4:6

The minute it became clear that there would be responsibilities along with this very sweet real estate deal, and that his own property might become entangled with that of Naomi's husband, the nameless other relative quickly bowed out.

By giving the man a chance to say yes or no to each part of the deal, Boaz was making sure that his own right to be the redeemer would not be challenged down the road. No one could say that Boaz had not presented each detail in order, without any confusion. This meant that no one in the future could challenge Ruth's legal status as his wife. By bringing extra clarity to the deal, Boaz was once again providing Ruth with protection. Boaz's last words in the book are spoken to the assembled elders at the city gate:

> Then Boaz announced to the elders and all the people, "Today you are witnesses that I have bought from Naomi all the property of Elimelek, Kilion and Mahlon. I have also acquired Ruth the Moabite, Mahlon's widow, as my wife, in order to maintain the name of the dead with his property, so that his name will not disappear from among his family or from his hometown. Today you are witnesses!"
> Ruth 4:9-10

This passage gives us yet another glimpse of the selflessness and kindness that characterized Boaz—one last look at the happy future that awaited these two kind and courageous people as they built a life together. When Boaz and the other relative had initially discussed the possibility of marrying Ruth, Boaz used the customary formula: "in order to maintain the name of the dead with his property." But in his public statement at the city gate, Boaz expanded on that. He went on to say, "so that his name will not disappear from among his family or from his hometown." He showed consideration for the family of Naomi, and for the memory of Elimelek, Kilion, and Mahlon. Instead of being threatened by their existence and their remembrance, he dedicated himself to helping to preserve them.

Ruth and Boaz were not star-crossed teenagers when God brought them to each other. Ruth arrived in Boaz's life carrying a painful past, which also probably included bittersweet memories of her marriage to her first husband. Boaz wasn't threatened by that. We know from his remarks to Ruth at the threshing floor that Boaz was older than she, not one of the "younger men." It would have been unusual in that day and time for a man of wealth and standing in the community to have reached middle age without being married, so it is possible—and even probable—that Boaz had been married before. This would mean that they both carried into their life together the memory of a life with another person and commitment to another person and even love with another person.

Ruth holds before us the tender reality and hope of widowed love—of second-chance love. The Bible tells us, in the story of these honorable people, that second love is never second-best love. The first love does not have to be erased, or belittled, or forgotten, in order for the second love to be true. Ruth changed and grew in the years after her marriage to Mahlon ended in heartbreak. Through her journey of grief, she once again found joy. Those who have known the loss of a previous love carry an awareness of sorrow joined to love, a memory of grief and loss. But sometimes God allows our hearts to break open in our sorrow so that He can pour more blessings inside.

There are few things that make me happier than seeing a widow or widower, or someone who has walked through a painful divorce, find a godly new spouse. It's certainly not the path for everyone, but it's a beautiful thing to witness when it happens—to see a devastated, broken heart brought back to life by a second chance. I've had a front-row seat to some of these love stories, and they fill me with optimism!

Boaz and Ruth's marriage wasn't just a second chance for the two of them. There was joy and redemption for Naomi too, long after she had assumed God had turned His back on her. She became a grandmother! Little baby Obed meant that her late husband's family name would live on. He would also be grandfather to David, a key link in the lineage that led to Christ our Savior (Matthew 1). Naomi's community, the one that she'd left in distress and returned to in despair, celebrated with her.

The women said to Naomi: "Praise be to the LORD, who this day has not left you without a guardian-redeemer. May he become famous throughout Israel! He will renew your life and sustain you in your old age. For your daughter-in-law, who loves you and who is better to you than seven sons, has given him birth."

Ruth 4:14–15

Naomi had gone home to Bethlehem certain that God had nothing good left for her. Little could she have known! It's a valuable reminder to all of us.

And we know that in all things God works for the good of those who love him, who have been called according to his purpose.
    Romans 8:28

From the early days of the church, Christian writers and commenters found deep meaning in the book of Ruth. The book was revered by Jews as the record of King David's ancestors. For Christians, Ruth was the account of the ancestors of Jesus, mentioned throughout the Gospels. Ruth pointed directly to Christ, but just as significantly she pointed to *Christians*. In the person of Ruth, a non-Jew who was joined to the people of God by her faith and devotion, Gentile Christians saw themselves. Gathered from among the nations to become part of the people of God, they too were foreigners like Ruth. They too had been called to a special purpose.

Boaz as a redeemer modeled what Christ would do for those outsiders. He stepped in to pay the price for each of us, when we were poor and in need. Much like Ruth, we cannot offer anything to our Redeemer but our devotion, integrity, and thanks. And like Boaz, Christ meets us with kindness and compassion, not chiding or turning us away for coming to Him. No. Like Boaz, Christ wraps His acceptance around us and gives us life anew—one full of second chances.

Prayer: Lord God, thank You for working even when we cannot see Your Hand through our own pain and loss.

Thank You for reminding us throughout Scripture that You are the God of second chances. Please help our eyes and hearts to be open to the evidence of Your work in the midst of our trials. Prompt us to give sacrificially to those in need in our lives, knowing that servanthood is what You call us to—and equip us to fulfill. May we cherish the gift of love.

The Rebel and the Peacemaker

1 Samuel 24–25

One of the Bible's most fascinating love stories is the one between David and Abigail. It's a drama that gets a lot less airtime than some of David's other, more high-profile romances—his marriage to Michal, King Saul's daughter, or his marriage to Bathsheba. Both of those relationships were marked by seasons of unhappiness and loss. After David fled Saul's court, one step ahead of the royal assassins, Saul took Michal and married her off to another man. Once again using her as a pawn for his purposes. When Michal was eventually returned to David, their relationship descended into acrimony and mutual contempt. David's relationship with Bathsheba began with adultery, murder, and the death of their child. Michal was granted to David more or less as a gift by her father, and Bathsheba was taken from her husband by David.

Abigail's relationship with David had a much different start. And the background of what happened before they met gives us important context. Long a faithful servant to Saul, David had also garnered a lot of attention and praise for his brave exploits as a warrior. Their relationship morphed into jealousy and rage as Saul increasingly viewed David as a threat, and set out to kill him—repeatedly. David spent years on the run from Saul, and it was during that time that he first crossed paths with Abigail in 1 Samuel 25.

But before we get to their introduction, let's recall what had happened just prior to that. Saul had taken 3,000 of his men and gone looking to murder David. At one point the king went into a cave to relieve himself, the same cave where David and his men were hiding (1 Samuel 24:3). The men actually urged David to turn the tables and take out Saul, but he did something very unusual instead—he cut off the corner of Saul's robe without the king noticing. David actually wound up feeling guilty about it.

> He said to his men, "The LORD forbid that I should do such a thing to my master, the LORD's anointed, or lay my hand on him; for he is the anointed of the LORD." With these words David sharply rebuked his men and did not allow them to attack Saul. And Saul left the cave and went his way.
> 1 Samuel 24:6-7

The man whose number one goal had become killing David was—in a most vulnerable moment—given a reprieve by David. This would not be the last time David would have an opportunity to take Saul's life, yet each time David deferred to God's anointment of Saul. He, too, could have easily followed the human impulses toward revenge or self-protection. David respected God's plan instead.

He did, however, try to use the situation to prove his loyalty to Saul.

Then David went out of the cave and called out to Saul, "My lord the king!" When Saul looked behind him, David bowed down and prostrated himself with his face to the ground. He said to Saul, "Why do you listen when men say, 'David is bent on harming you'? This day you have seen with your own eyes how the LORD delivered you into my hands in the cave. Some urged me to kill you, but I spared you; I said, 'I will not lay my hand on my lord, because he is the LORD's anointed.' See, my father, look at this piece of your robe in my hand! I cut off the corner of your robe but did not kill you. See that there is nothing in my hand to indicate that I am guilty of wrongdoing or rebellion. I have not wronged you, but you are hunting me down to take my life."
1 Samuel 24:8–11

Saul "wept aloud" and confessed to David, "You are more righteous than I." (1 Samuel 24:17) He also asked the Lord to "reward" David for the way he had spared Saul's life. Then, the king himself added this prophecy:

I know that you will surely be king and that the kingdom of Israel will be established in your hands.
1 Samuel 24:20

Was it precisely because Saul was so aware of that coming reality that he became obsessed with destroying David before he could assume the throne? This moment when Saul took in the reality of how easily David could have killed him shows us he was still human, capable of remorse and compassion despite his periodic bouts of mental instability and violence.

Saul asked David to swear an oath to him before the Lord, that David would never wipe out his descendants or family name. Scripture tells us David made the oath (not that Saul promised anything to him) and the two men went their separate ways. And that's when the story takes us to David and Abigail's meeting.

> **Then David moved down into the Desert of Paran. A certain man in Maon, who had property there at Carmel, was very wealthy. He had a thousand goats and three thousand sheep, which he was shearing in Carmel. His name was Nabal and his wife's name was Abigail. She was an intelligent and beautiful woman, but her husband was surly and mean in his dealings—he was a Calebite.**
> **1 Samuel 25:2–3**

A thousand goats and three thousand sheep would make him the equivalent of a multimillionaire—certainly one of the richest men in the kingdom. And while he may have been wealthy in terms of possessions, it sounds like he was poor in character: "surly and mean." How would you like to be described that way for all time? By contrast, Abigail is described as intelligent and beautiful. The Hebrew word for intelligence here is *sekhel,* and this is the only time in the Bible it's used to describe a woman. It means one has an excellent sense of something or wise discretion. We'll soon see how well that fits Abigail.

The timing of this meeting is also crucial. It was sheep-shearing season, which was considered a festive time. There were often feasts and celebrations to commemorate the profits flock owners would collect after the hard work of the breeding season.

David must have sensed this would be a good time to approach Nabal, to highlight the work David and his men had done in protecting Nabal's valuable flocks.

> So he sent ten young men and said to them, "Go up to Nabal at Carmel and greet him in my name. Say to him: 'Long life to you! Good health to you and your household! And good health to all that is yours! Now I hear that it is sheep-shearing time. When your shepherds were with us, we did not mistreat them, and the whole time they were at Carmel nothing of theirs was missing. Ask your own servants and they will tell you. Therefore be favorable toward my men, since we come at a festive time. Please give your servants and your son David whatever you can find for them.'"
> 1 Samuel 25:5–8

David sent greetings and good wishes to Nabal and everything under his watch. He also politely reminded Nabal of the service he and his men had provided—and that they'd done it with integrity. David referred to his men as Nabal's "servants," and asked for anything the wealthy man saw as appropriate reward. There were no demands.

David's use of the words "your son" were also a show of reverence to the older, established man. This was the way things worked in the ancient world. David would have had reason to offer protection to Nabal's shepherds against Philistine attacks in the area. David and his band of heavily armed men could have easily stolen some of Nabal's sheep for their own provisions. David and

his men were living close to the bone in those days, always looking for ways to feed themselves, and taking a few sheep here and
there would have been understandable. But David had refrained.
He had performed a valuable service for Nabal, and with great
respect and good wishes David went to Nabal for compensation.

Things did not however go exactly to plan. Nabal first feigned
ignorance of the young man whose reputation was likely known
widely throughout the land.

> **Nabal answered David's servants, "Who is this David? Who
> is this son of Jesse? Many servants are breaking away from
> their masters these days. Why should I take my bread and
> water, and the meat I have slaughtered for my shearers,
> and give it to men coming from who knows where?"**
> **1 Samuel 25:10–11**

David's just and righteous action had been met with ingrat-
itude. Worse, David was deeply insulted. "Many servants are
breaking away from their masters these days," Nabal said, taking
a dig at David with regard to King Saul. Never mind that David
had always conducted himself uprightly with Saul. Nabal was
classifying David (whom he'd pretended he hadn't even heard
of) as Saul's servant—essentially a nobody from nowhere. Nabal's
harsh comeback stood in stark contrast to David's respectful approach and deference.

When David's men came back to him with Nabal's response,
he was not amused.

> **David said to his men, "Each of you strap on your sword!"**
> **So they did, and David strapped his on as well. About four**

hundred men went up with David, while two hundred stayed with the supplies.

1 Samuel 25:13

David's respect for the Lord's anointed might have kept him from bearing arms against Saul, but in that moment of rage there was nothing to stop him from teaching Nabal a lesson. This was no small band of hillside bandits, quite the contrary. David commanded about 600 men, hardened warriors who had gone into battle with him and who had staked everything on his eventual triumph as king. If they were going to pay Nabal a visit, it would not be to threaten him; it would be to execute him and every member of his household.

A warning about the impending payback came from within Nabal's own home.

One of the servants told Abigail, Nabal's wife, "David sent messengers from the wilderness to give our master his greetings, but he hurled insults at them. Yet these men were very good to us. They did not mistreat us, and the whole time we were out in the fields near them nothing was missing. Night and day they were a wall around us the whole time we were herding our sheep near them. Now think it over and see what you can do, because disaster is hanging over our master and his whole household. He is such a wicked man that no one can talk to him."

1 Samuel 25:14–17

This interaction suggests that Nabal's own servants were aware of just how hotheaded he could be, and that Abigail was capable of wisely seeing the way to defusing the situation. Maybe she'd played this role with her husband before. The servant did say Nabal was so wicked that no one could reason with him.

Here we see Abigail's response is the one of someone who is wise and resourceful. Did she run to Nabal to chew him out? No doubt she knew that would be a fruitless mission. Scripture tells us she "acted quickly" (1 Samuel 25:18), and put together a massive feast of wine, bread, meat, and cakes and hurried out to meet David. "But she did not tell her husband Nabal." (1 Samuel 25:19b) Remember that description of her: wise discretion.

We've all been put into pressure-cooker situations where tact and prudence can be our greatest assets. Imagine finding out that 400 warriors are headed your way to wipe out your entire household. Would you panic? Meltdown? Or would you pull an Abigail and start preparing to intercede with grace and humility? She assembled all the offerings that Nabal should have, and went on offense. All the wealth that her husband ought to have shared so generously, Abigail took upon herself to offer.

If Nabal's servants wanted justice done, they knew better than to approach Nabal. They went directly to Abigail, who was the one in the family capable of sound judgment. From the details we glean about Abigail in 1 Samuel we see many parallels with the capable wife often described as an ideal in Proverbs 31. For one thing, she was trying to save Nabal's neck

> She brings him good, not harm,
>   all the days of her life.
>   Proverbs 31:12

Scripture also portrays Abigail as someone those closest to her trusted and respected.

> She speaks with wisdom,
>   and faithful instruction is on her tongue.
> She watches over the affairs of her household
>   and does not eat the bread of idleness.
> Proverbs 31:26–27

Boy, was she ever watching over the affairs of her household! It all begs the question about how much of Nabal's success might have been—at least in part—the result of his wife's wisdom and advice.

It brings to mind the guidance in another well-known Proverb.

> A gentle answer turns away wrath,
>   but a harsh word stirs up anger.
> Proverbs 15:1

Nabal had done one of these, and Abigail would literally save their lives by offering up the other.

We're told nothing about the actual marriage or personal relationship of Nabal and Abigail; we don't have to be detectives to guess that it probably wasn't great. But what a powerful picture of how an astute wife could make the very best of her less-than-ideal circumstances. Abigail could have simply resigned herself to the fact that Nabal was constantly going to be putting them in danger or causing conflict. In those days he would have been the clear leader of their household, and she could have chosen to stand back and allow his rude behavior to create serious consequences for all of them. But it's evident her *sekhel* intelligence would not allow her to cower. Instead, she took action and wisely approached David with both generous blessings and a contrite attitude.

> When Abigail saw David, she quickly got off her donkey and bowed down before David with her face to the ground. She fell at his feet and said: "Pardon your servant, my lord, and let me speak to you; hear what your servant has to say. Please pay no attention, my lord, to that wicked man Nabal. He is just like his name—his name means Fool, and folly goes with him. And as for me, your servant, I did not see the men my lord sent."
>
> 1 Samuel 25:23-25

Abigail immediately showed David the exact opposite of what he'd gotten from Nabal's insulting response: respect.

It's interesting to look at how some other translations describe her initial words to David. "Upon me, my lord, upon me let this iniquity be . . ." (King James Version). "My master, let me take the blame!" (The Message). "On me alone, my lord, be the guilt" (English Standard Version). Abigail had done nothing wrong, yet she asked David to allow her to bear Nabal's guilt in order to save all those under the care of her household. What a beautiful foreshadowing of what we would eventually see Christ do for all of us centuries later. Just as man sinned against God and created a spiritual crisis, Nabal had offended David—who was looking for payback. Just as Abigail sought to pay the price for her rotten husband, Christ stood in the gap for every human being who would ever need rescue—everyone of us! It wasn't a sentence imposed upon Him, but one that He willingly took on in order to make eternal peace between God and man. Where Abigail likely saved dozens, Christ redeemed an infinite number of desperate souls.

Abigail's opening plea also acknowledged her husband's faults: wickedness and folly. She immediately signaled to David that he—the future king—was to be exalted, and she continued.

> And now, my lord, as surely as the LORD your God lives and as you live, since the LORD has kept you from bloodshed and from avenging yourself with your own hands, may your enemies and all who are intent on harming my lord be like Nabal. And let this gift, which your servant has brought to my lord, be given to the men who follow you.
>
> 1 Samuel 25: 26–27

Abigail declared the existence and glory of God, and noted His favor to David. She also shrewdly credited God with keeping David from wiping out Nabal's entire household. Abigail then offered the lavish gifts David was already due.

Abigail also went several steps further, proclaiming that the Lord would "make a lasting dynasty" for David (1 Samuel 25:28), and that no wrongdoing would be found in David because he was fighting the Lord's battles. She showed an impressive awareness about David's past, as well as David's present. Look at what she said about God's protection of David: "Even though someone is pursuing you to take your life, the life of my lord will be bound securely in the bundle of the living by the LORD your God, but the lives of your enemies he will hurl away as from the pocket of a sling." (1 Samuel 25:29)

Who could be the one pursuing David to take his life but Saul? Abigail was clearly aware that David was running for his life, and that Saul wanted him dead. But she also knew David's past, and she honored him by recalling his most famous exploit when she said the lives of David's enemies would be hurled away "as from the pocket of a sling." David was the slingshot warrior, the one who killed Goliath with a single well-aimed shot. By giving this past exploit a subtle shout-out, Abigail both honored David and, not incidentally, reminded him how unworthy an opponent the boorish Nabal would be.

She also masterfully outlined for David that by sparing Nabal's life he wouldn't later bear the guilt of the obnoxious man's destruction once he—David—became king.

> When the LORD has fulfilled for my lord every good thing he promised concerning him and has appointed him ruler over Israel, my lord will not have on his conscience the staggering burden of needless bloodshed or of having avenged himself. And when the LORD your God has brought my lord success, remember your servant.
> 1 Samuel 25:30–31

Abigail's speech is a masterful example of persuasive oratory. How many modern-day disasters could we avoid in our own lives if we simply took the time to reach out with humility and grace? Think about how angry or hurt you've been when an insult or slight trickled back to you through secondhand whispers. *Is that what the person actually said? Were they misinformed about something you'd said first?* I've seen enough reality TV to know that when you go in for a confrontation—guns blazing (and isn't that exactly what the producers want?)—it's hard to put the tooth-paste back in the tube. One of the nipped-and-tucked housewives (often tipsy and goaded by another one of the women) runs bar-reling into a crowded party and starts blasting an unsuspecting third party about something it turns out (whoops—roll the tape) the person maybe never actually said.

Abigail did none of this. She knew exactly what Nabal had said and done, and she assumed the best about David and appealed to his respect for God. Abigail expressed wholehearted belief in David. She treated him like the king she was confident he would be. The ancient rabbis counted Abigail among the prophets for this moment because she foretold David's triumph with such cer-tainty, and acted in the faith that it would occur.

In return, Abigail requested one thing. She asked David to re-member her—to have continued mercy on her and her household. She took her place in this complicated network of gratitude and repayment. David was deferential to Nabal; Nabal was ungrateful to David. Abigail was respectful to David, and David (she hoped) would be gracious to her. Again and again she proved the use of the word *sekhel* to describe her was accurate; she was worthy of it. It is easy to imagine David, the forthright warrior, standing there slack-jawed and amazed at Abigail's verbal pyrotechnics. What must he have made of her? She was probably unlike anything he had ever seen before—in her brilliance, her courage, and her in-dependence.

David said to Abigail, "Praise be to the Lord, the God of Israel, who has sent you today to meet me. May you be blessed for your good judgment and for keeping me from bloodshed this day and from avenging myself with my own hands. Otherwise, as surely as the LORD, the God of Israel, lives, who has kept me from harming you, if you had not come quickly to meet me, not one male belonging to Nabal would have been left alive by daybreak."

Then David accepted from her hand what she had brought him and said, "Go home in peace. I have heard your words and granted your request."

1 Samuel 25: 32-35

He praised her "good judgment," and thanked her for intervening—for keeping him from bloodshed and revenge. David's positive response was not a foregone conclusion. Abigail took a risk in doing what she did, because it wasn't outside the realm of possibility that David would reprove or rebuke her for directly approaching him—especially without the approval of her husband. In those days it could very easily have been viewed as insubordination to Nabal. David could very well have chastised Abigail for her disloyalty or turned on her. But he didn't. He listened and praised God for her prescience and her words.

Abigail must have rushed home in great relief, having averted certain disaster for all Nabal held dear. When she got there, 1 Samuel 25:36 tells us Nabal was living it up, "holding a banquet like that of a king." Those words struck me the first time I read them in the context of this story. David had actually been anointed king. He would be the leader of Israel, chosen directly by God. Nabal in his greed and arrogance had sent David's men away with contempt. So while Abigail was out negotiating the peace with (future king) David, Nabal was at home acting like *he* was royalty. The contrast with David must have been painfully clear: a brave, principled warrior on the one hand and a mean, drunken jerk on the other. It's not surprising that Abigail surveyed the situation and decided not to tell Nabal what she'd done until the next day.

> Then in the morning, when Nabal was sober, his wife told him all these things, and his heart failed him and he became like a stone.
> 1 Samuel 25:37

It took courage to face Nabal, and to own up to what she had undertaken. He might have been mean and pathetic, but he was her husband. Nabal would have held all the cards in that time and place. He could have chastised his wife, or much worse. He does seem like the kind of man who would have acted impetuously, one whose pride likely would have been wounded very easily. Abigail could have hidden her pleas to David and the gifts she took. Remember, the servant worried about David coming to kill them hadn't gone to Nabal. He'd taken the terrifying truth to the lady of the house. But she waited until her husband could fully understand what she was saying, and only then related the whole story about her trip to meet David and his men.

Though we're not entirely sure what happened to Nabal, most scholars believe he suffered a heart attack or a stroke. Was he just taking in the reality that he and his household had come this close to death? Was he stunned that his wife had maneuvered around him and saved them all? Whatever shocked him had a serious physical impact. He "became like a stone," which could be a description of him falling into a coma. It wouldn't last.

> About ten days later, the LORD struck Nabal and he died.
> 1 Samuel 25:38

Make no mistake here, God meted out punishment to Nabal. It cost the wicked, selfish man his life. Though David burned with anger at the insults leveled at him and his men by Nabal, Abigail's words and humble approach stopped him from slaughtering their household. When David stood down, God settled the account.

David immediately praised the Lord—just as he had thanked Abigail—for keeping him from sin and regret in the midst of his fury.

> When David heard that Nabal was dead, he said, "Praise be to the LORD, who has upheld my cause against Nabal for treating me with contempt. He has kept his servant from doing wrong and has brought Nabal's wrongdoing down on his own head."
> 1 Samuel 25:39a

David wasted no time in keeping his promise to Abigail, and you better believe he remembered her.

> Then David sent word to Abigail, asking her to become his wife.
> 1 Samuel 25:39b

Plot twist! This woman described as both intelligent and beautiful made quite an impression on David. He had seen her discretion and humility in action. She showed him respect and acknowledged his destiny as God's chosen king.

His servants went to Carmel and said to Abigail, "David has sent us to you to take you to become his wife." She bowed down with her face to the ground and said, "I am your servant and am ready to serve you and wash the feet of my lord's servants." Abigail quickly got on a donkey and, attended by her five female servants, went with David's messengers and became his wife.

1 Samuel 25: 40–42

What a turn of events for this wise woman, who had likely been Nabal's best asset. Though she'd been married to an unkind, haughty man she had acted quickly—with solid judgment—under pressure. To a future king on the run for his life, she was a godsend. We can imagine that she felt the same way about David.

David had likely seen many beautiful women both inside the palace and out, but Abigail's intelligence must have served to captivate David in a wholly different way. Her powerful way with words made him see himself and his actions in a new light. It was her sage counsel that saved him from giving in to his anger and offended pride. David was, after all, more than just a warrior. He was also a talented musician and writer of songs and laments. It's easy to imagine that Abigail's impassioned rhetoric impressed David.

So often in looking at love stories, we focus on the happiness of two people. But Abigail and David's story also gives us a look at a difficult marriage, one in which a wife was sent scrambling on a life-saving mission because of her husband's rude arrogance. It's unlikely that Abigail had much choice about her marriage to Nabal, but she didn't wither under his shameful behavior. She was clearly resourceful and trusted by the people of her household. She had found a way to flourish in the midst of a problematic marriage. It's a reality that's not uncommon for many spouses. I often say (half-jokingly) that if you've been married for longer than five minutes you probably need a counselor or therapist. That's just life! But something tells me Nabal wouldn't have been eager to sign up for marriage counseling.

God is most certainly the God of second chances, whether that's healing a broken marriage or releasing you from one that has destroyed the biblical boundaries He set for us. As a very little girl I distinctly remember there were some people in church who treated my mom as a sort of second-class Christian because of her divorce from my father. There's an infinite amount they could not have known about exactly what happened between the two of them. Even as a kid I experienced sadness over the shame I sometimes felt because of the way some people viewed our situation. But others embraced her with open hearts, and we knew that God had never abandoned us.

Just as Abigail found a new chapter with David, so my mom found happiness and spiritual strength in her marriage to my stepfather. God wasn't done with her story. In fact, it was just beginning in so many ways! We know that the Lord can take what the enemy intends for evil and turn it to good (Genesis 50:20). He certainly did that for Abigail. Her righteous and compassionate action impacted the course of David's life—which is to say, she changed the course of Israel's history, and ours.

Prayer: Heavenly Father, please gift us with Your wisdom and discernment in every challenge we face. Help us to be humble, but willing to step in and act to right a wrong. Please show us, LORD, how to make peace and bring harmony in the midst of chaos and injustice. Remind us that we are not powerless in the midst of trouble, that You equip and guide us. You are the God of second chances.

FRIENDSHIP LOVE

Proverbs 18:24 tells us "there is a friend who sticks closer than a brother," and in the stories ahead you'll see that reality played out across the pages of the Old and New Testaments. I often thank God for what I believe are some of His kindest, most generous earthly gifts: soulmate friends. While romantic love may grab the headlines, for most of us it's the daily support and encouragement of our friends that fuels us.

My childhood friend Julie and I used to dress in matching blue and white checked dresses and sing duets everywhere from

Sunday School to the race track (long story). And I have the most vivid memories of my middle school bestie, Michelle, and I making our annual multicolored Christmas cookies. There was also that all-night slumber party at Tara's after she scored a copy of Michael Jackson's *Thriller* album. It was heavy on dancing and squealing, not so much on the slumbering.

As I ventured into my college years, it was my friends who showed up when my heart got broken and when I somehow wound up on the stage at Miss America. They were there to encourage my fondest dreams, and to pick up the pieces when things didn't go as planned. What a treasure to still have so many of them in my life! We've all gotten older, traversed some gut-wrenching tragedies, spoken truth to each other and celebrated a growing list of milestones. God gifted me with each of these confidants, just as we see Him do for His children throughout Scripture. And even in their imperfection, our friendships can point us to Him.

DAVID AND JONATHAN

Brothers in Arms

> 1 Samuel 17–18:9, 19:1–7, 20:1–42,
> 23:15–18, 2 Samuel 1:22–27, 9:1–11

It's not surprising after the leadership of a series of judges, including the flawed and chaotic years of Samson, that the people of Israel were antsy about wanting something different. So they complained and demanded that God give them a king. They wanted to be like everyone else. But Israel's mistake throughout the Old Testament was to look for stability in human leaders instead of their God. In essence they were dismissing their heavenly king for a fallible, earthly one. He told the prophet Samuel, "They have rejected me as their king." (1 Samuel 8:7b) God told Samuel to caution the people about exactly who and what they were getting and what it would cost them, and added:

> When that day comes, you will cry out for relief from the king you have chosen, but the LORD will not answer you in that day.
> 1 Samuel 8:18

Still they insisted to Samuel, they wanted a king like all the other nations and God gave them one.

In fact, He gave them a king who must have seemed like the monarch of their dreams, "as handsome a young man as could be found anywhere" and "a head taller than anyone else" in Israel (1 Samuel 9:2). Suddenly, the new guy in charge was George Clooney! (It's just that he turned out to be doofus George Clooney in *O Brother Where Art Thou* instead of suave Clooney in *Oceans Eleven*.) In the years after God appointed Saul as the first king of Israel, it became increasingly obvious that Saul had serious character flaws and mental health issues. He was paranoid and fearful, a people pleaser who would do anything to be liked, including ignoring God's commands.

But another theme in this time in Israel's history is the stark difference that sometimes existed between fathers and sons. Saul's oldest son, Jonathan, had all the positive qualities his father lacked: nobility, faith, courage, and humility. In fact, he sounded like he would someday be the ideal king. But God had a different path for Jonathan, whom we remember now as one of the most devoted friends in the Bible. A man willing to break with his own father in order to pledge an unwavering commitment to his best friend, David.

Today, our Western culture tends to prioritize romantic love above all other kinds of relationships. The love and fidelity of friendships can often be relegated to a kind of "runner-up" status in the sweepstakes of love. That view would have been very odd to someone in biblical times. In the ancient world, those values of commitment and devotion were almost reversed. Friendship was often seen as the most important kind of relationship, and romantic love was a distant second. In those days, marriage was largely about obligation, but friendship was about choice. Many people in the ancient world valued friendship over marriage because their culture viewed marriage as a legal agreement primarily dealing with the transfer of property and assets. In David and Jonathan's friendship we see two people vowing to have each other's backs in very difficult circumstances, not because of obligation—but by choice.

The Prince and the Pauper

David and Jonathan grew up in starkly different worlds. Jonathan's father was the king of Israel, and he was raised as a prince. Jonathan was expected to succeed his father as king one day, and once we get to know him—boy, does he stand in contrast to his hesitant, vain father. First Samuel 13 begins by mentioning Jonathan successfully leading men into battle under Saul's guidance. But our first in-depth introduction to Jonathan comes after Saul had failed to follow God's commands and was rejected by Him.

Saul was reluctant to engage the Philistine army, aware that they were better armed than his 600 men. (1 Samuel 13:19–22 reveals that the Israelites had to go to the Philistines to find blacksmiths to sharpen their own weapons!) Scripture tells us Saul was hanging out under a pomegranate tree (1 Samuel 14:8), but Jonathan was anxious to take on the Philistines. He was an experienced warrior and a skilled archer (2 Samuel 1:22). As his father hemmed and hawed, Jonathan decided to take along his armor-bearer and sneak his way into Philistine territory and spring a surprise attack. Together they navigated a path between two treacherous cliffs, as Jonathan asked the Lord for a sign about how to proceed. With that guidance clear, the two men proceeded to wipe out the Philistine enemies who had challenged them to come up and get "a lesson." (1 Samuel 14:12) The experience shows us both Jonathan's bravery and humility in seeking God's wisdom and favor.

David's start in life would have been decidedly different, but we can see early parallels between Jonathan's courage and David's. David's father, Jesse, appears to have been a prosperous farmer, but a farmer is not a king. As the youngest son, David would have had more than his fair share of chores, and he occupied the lowest rung in the family hierarchy. He spent most of his youth as a shepherd—living on the hillsides with his father's flocks. Looking after the herds was an important task because so much of the family's property was tied up in the flocks, but it was also dangerous, lonely work far from the center of any action.

It was in those fields that David was hiding in plain sight when God directed Samuel to go and find Israel's new king. Samuel was sent to Jesse and he considered his sons one by one. The Lord told him none of those contenders was the chosen one. Finally, David was called in from tending the flocks, and God immediately told Samuel the youngest of Jesse's sons was the one.

> So Samuel took the horn of oil and anointed him in the presence of his brothers, and from that day on the Spirit of the LORD came powerfully upon David.
> 1 Samuel 16:13

Not long after that, Saul began to be tormented and asked his attendants to locate someone to play music to comfort him. They found David, who quickly became a fixture in the palace. It's highly possible David crossed paths with Jonathan during that time, but the first time we witness a formal meeting between the two is in the valley of Elah. That's where Saul and his men were camped out awaiting battle with the Philistines and their champion, Goliath.

First Samuel 17 is where we find the thrilling story of David's insistence that he—a young fighter with no formal training—should be the one to confront the nearly ten-foot-tall Goliath. Even as King Saul tried to talk him out of it, David made his case—talking about the wild animals he'd fought off with his bare hands as he protected his father's flocks. When David finally got past all the objections and naysayers he stood to face Goliath.

> David said to the Philistine, "You come against me with sword and spear and javelin, but I come against you in the name of the LORD Almighty, the God of the armies of Israel, whom you have defied. This day the LORD will deliver you into my hands, and I'll strike you down and cut off your head. This very day I will give the carcasses of the Philistine army to the birds and the wild animals, and the whole world will know that there is a God in Israel. All those gathered here will know that it is not by sword or spear that the LORD saves; for the battle is the LORD's, and he will give all of you into our hands."
>
> 1 Samuel 17:45–47

Just as Jonathan had done, David charged right into battle—trusting God to guide and protect him. He took down Goliath and was summoned by Saul.

After David had finished talking with Saul, Jonathan became one in spirit with David, and he loved him as himself. From that day Saul kept David with him and did not
let him return home to his family. And Jonathan made
a covenant with David because he loved him as himself.
Jonathan took off the robe he was wearing and gave it to
David, along with his tunic, and even his sword, his bow
and his belt.

1 Samuel 18:1–4

As the eldest son of the king, it would have been expected that
Jonathan was next in line to the throne. But instead of viewing
David as some kind of threat to Saul or to himself, it seems Jonathan felt an immediate kinship with this young warrior. Neither
had been willing to wait for Saul to act when the Philistines were
threatening. Both had trusted the Lord and gone on offense.
Could Jonathan already see God's anointing on David? In any
case, their bond was quick and lasting.

Is there a friendship in your life that felt instant from the very
beginning? We occasionally have those life moments of, "This
person gets me and I get her!" Years ago when I took a report-
ing and anchoring job in Washington, DC, I was paired up with
someone I wouldn't meet until after she returned from maternity
leave. From the moment I finally got to meet Eun we realized we
were basically the same human being split into two different bodies. We had so much fun from day one that we were constantly
chided by our stage managers who were terrified we'd be caught
deep in a debate about some reality TV show when the *actual*
TV newscast we were doing came back from commercial. We in-
stantly bonded over our love for Jesus, fashion magazines, and

junk food. There was no ice to be broken. I can't remember one moment she didn't feel like a sister to me. I've often joked we were separated at birth, which always provokes some very confused responses on social media—given that she's Korean-American and I'm obviously not!

Jonathan and David forged a deep friendship under much different circumstances, but just as I would do anything for Eun and know she would also for me—these two friends were in it for life. As Saul grew to be jealous of David in the years that followed, Jonathan only grew in his admiration and respect for his loyal friend. Because of Jonathan's friendship with David, David's life would be saved when Saul eventually turned on him. David's survival meant he was able to one day become king of Israel and the ancestor of Christ—meaning one of the reasons you and I are Christians today is the faithful friendship of David and Jonathan.

Some of the language the Bible uses to describe David and Jonathan may seem unusual to us. What does it mean to say that Jonathan "became one in spirit" with David? The Hebrew verb *kashar* (or *qashar*) means to link, or to tie, and the phrase literally says that "the spirit of Jonathan was tied to the spirit of David." It's interesting that it doesn't say *"he* tied his spirit to David's." This link was something that happened *to* them. This is the same verb that appears in Deuteronomy, when Moses told the children of Israel to "fix these words of mine in your hearts and minds; *tie* them as symbols on your hands and bind them on your foreheads." (Deuteronomy 11:18) Jonathan's soul was tied to David's just as the words of God were tied to the children of Israel, which tells us something about the holiness and depth of their friendship.

God Himself is in a friendship with each of us as believers. Abraham's relationship with God represents the old covenant. James 2:23 tells us, "He was called God's friend." Jesus ushered in the new covenant centuries later.

> I no longer call you servants, because a servant does not know his master's business. Instead, I have called you friends, for everything that I learned from my Father I have made known to you.
> John 15:15

We can have no better ally or friend!

After David's triumph over Goliath, Saul kept David close and did not let him return home. Was Saul determined to honor David, to essentially adopt him as a prince in his household? Or did he already (wrongly) view David as a threat to be monitored? Regardless of Saul's motivation we soon see, "whatever mission Saul sent him on, David was so successful that Saul gave him a high rank in the army." (1 Samuel 18:5) Was Saul himself conflicted about David and his role in the kingdom? We soon get our answer.

> When the men were returning home after David had killed the Philistine, the women came out from all the towns of Israel to meet King Saul with singing and dancing, with joyful songs and with timbrels and lyres. As they danced, they sang:
>
> "Saul has slain his thousands,
> and David his tens of thousands."
>
> Saul was very angry; this refrain displeased him greatly. "They have credited David with tens of thousands," he

thought, "but me with only thousands. What more can he get but the kingdom?"

And from that time on Saul kept a close eye on David.

1 Samuel 18:6–9

Whatever jealousy stirred in Saul's heart, his son Jonathan felt none of it. Again and again we will see their covenant of selfless friendship renewed.

Peacemaking

Saul wasn't content to simply keep an eye on David. The king actually tried to use his daughter as a pawn in his psychotic plans to harm David. Saul knew his younger daughter, Michal, was in love with David and saw an opportunity.

"I will give her to him," he thought, "so that she may be a snare to him and so that the hand of the Philistines may be against him."

1 Samuel 18:21a

Saul then gave David what he probably thought was a death sentence: go kill 100 Philistines in exchange for my daughter's hand. Instead, David and his men killed 200 Philistines. Saul knew he was in trouble.

When Saul realized that the LORD was with David and that his daughter Michal loved David, Saul became still more

afraid of him, and he remained his enemy the rest of his
days.

1 Samuel 18:28-29

Saul actively sought ways not simply to marginalize David,
but to murder him. That forced the king's own son to take sides.

Saul told his son Jonathan and all the attendants to kill
David. But Jonathan had taken a great liking to David and
warned him, "My father Saul is looking for a chance to kill
you. Be on your guard tomorrow morning; go into hiding
and stay there. I will go out and stand with my father in
the field where you are. I'll speak to him about you and
will tell you what I find out." Jonathan spoke well of David to Saul his father and said to him, "Let not the king do
wrong to his servant David; he has not wronged you, and
what he has done has benefited you greatly. He took his
life in his hands when he killed the Philistine. The LORD
won a great victory for all Israel, and you saw it and were
glad. Why then would you do wrong to an innocent man
like David by killing him for no reason?"

1 Samuel 19: 1-5

Jonathan tried to defend his friend, and he did something
understandable: He tried to reconcile the two people arguably most important in his life. Rather than plotting an escape
for David, Jonathan tried to find a way to keep him safely in the
king's court. When the text says Jonathan had taken a great liking to David, the original wording means to delight in someone.
When Caleb and Joshua were exhorting the people of Israel to

take heart, they told them that "if the Lord is pleased with us, he will lead us into that land, a land flowing with milk and honey." (Numbers 14:8) The verb used for the Lord's delight in and pleasure with His people is the same verb used here for Jonathan's bond with his friend. It's a word that has to do with the *joy* at the heart of a friendship—the comfort we feel in shared memories and time together.

In this conversation with his father, Jonathan modeled how we should advocate for our friends. Are we passionate, committed defenders who will speak up on their behalf? Do we keep our mouths shut if things get awkward, or do we boldly make the case on behalf of those closest to our heart? Jonathan showed vocal advocacy, especially when David wasn't there to champion himself.

Jonathan's persuasion of his father was successful—for a time. Saul swore, "As the Lord lives, David will not be put to death," (1 Samuel 19:6) and Jonathan was satisfied. Pleased that he had restored peace to the royal household, Jonathan told David everything that had been said. Jonathan brought his beloved friend into his father's presence, "and David was with Saul as before."

Separation

Sadly, Jonathan's victory was short-lived. His father quickly lapsed again into madness and homicidal rage, consumed with jealousy over David's military prowess. This time, he put his murderous intentions into action, and David barely escaped with his life. Saul first tried to spear David himself (1 Samuel 19:9–10), and then sent his men to David's home with orders to kill him. David's wife, Jonathan's sister, Michal—hatched a plan and sent her husband on the run. David hid away with the prophet Samuel, who had anointed him, and once again Saul sent his men after them. Multiple times, Saul sent his men to David and Samuel and they all ended being overcome with God's spirit. Saul finally went to see for himself, and God's spirit overtook him as well!

David was soon on the run once again, and got to his closest confidant—Jonathan. David begged Jonathan to tell him how he had wronged Saul, and asked why Saul was determined to take his life.

> "Never!" Jonathan replied. "You are not going to die! Look, my father doesn't do anything, great or small, without letting me know. Why would he hide this from me? It isn't so!" But David took an oath and said, "Your father knows very well that I have found favor in your eyes, and he has said to himself, 'Jonathan must not know this or he will be grieved.' Yet as surely as the LORD lives and as you live, there is only a step between me and death."
>
> 1 Samuel 20:2-3

It seems Jonathan had a hard time accepting that his father, Israel's king, could actually be trying to murder his best friend. David had to present Jonathan with an unpleasant truth—that Saul knew how close they were and it would only make sense that he would hide his intentions from his son. Jonathan didn't question David or call him a liar. Instead he said simply, "Whatever you want me to do, I'll do for you." (1 Samuel 20:4)

The two men then hatched an elaborate plan that would force Jonathan to press his own father for information about his intentions regarding David. It's here again that we see the unshakable commitment to their friendship as David pours out his heart to Jonathan.

> "As for you, show kindness to your servant, for you have brought him into a covenant with you before the LORD. If I am guilty, then kill me yourself! Why hand me over to your father?"
>
> "Never!" Jonathan said. "If I had the least inkling that my father was determined to harm you, wouldn't I tell you?"
>
> 1 Samuel 20:8–9

Jonathan then devised a way to send a message to David by way of arrows he would launch after speaking with Saul. Jonathan was willing to undermine his own maniacal father in order to save his best friend and honor their pledge. He then asked for David's protection for him and his family, in a way that certainly made it sound like he could imagine his dearest friend as a future king.

> But show me unfailing kindness like the Lord's kindness as long as I live, so that I may not be killed, and do not ever cut off your kindness from my family—not even when the Lord has cut off every one of David's enemies from the face of the earth.
>
> 1 Samuel 20:14–16

Before they put their plan into action, they reaffirmed—no matter what the outcome—their covenant with each other. Here we see one of the Bible's most beautiful affirmations of friendship:

> So Jonathan made a covenant with the house of David, saying, "May the LORD call David's enemies to account." And Jonathan had David reaffirm his oath out of love for him, because he loved him as he loved himself.
> 1 Samuel 20:16–17

And it didn't take long for it to be put to the test. In yet another attempt by Jonathan to protect David against Saul's rage, the bitter truth was revealed—from the king's own mouth.

> You son of a perverse and rebellious woman! Don't I know that you have sided with the son of Jesse to your own shame and to the shame of the mother who bore you? As long as the son of Jesse lives on this earth, neither you nor your kingdom will be established. Now send someone to bring him to me, for he must die!
> 1 Samuel 20:30–31

That was it, in a nutshell. Supporting David meant Jonathan was giving up the throne. But Jonathan was completely unfazed by that prospect. A godly man, he had accepted the word of God a long time ago. Unlike his father, Jonathan knew God would take the throne from the house of Saul.

> "Why should he be put to death? What has he done?" Jonathan asked his father. But Saul hurled his spear at him to

kill him. Then Jonathan knew that his father intended to kill David.

1 Samuel 20:32-33

Saul wasn't acting out of love for his family, but in anger fueled by his own pride. He too had chosen sides, and it wasn't with his own son. Jonathan left the table in anger and grief. In the morning he would send his arrows in a message of warning to David.

Having telegraphed to David that he wasn't safe, the two could have parted without saying goodbye. But David couldn't bear to escape without a thank-you to his closest friend—the person he trusted with his very life. So David emerged from his hiding place of safety.

...David got up from the south side of the stone and bowed down before Jonathan three times, with his face to the ground. Then they kissed each other and wept together— but David wept the most.

Jonathan said to David, "Go in peace, for we have sworn friendship with each other in the name of the LORD, saying, 'The LORD is witness between you and me, and between your descendants and my descendants forever.'" Then David left, and Jonathan went back to the town.

1 Samuel 20:41-42

David bowed before Jonathan, in overwhelming gratitude for what had just been done and what Jonathan had risked for him and in honor of his princely friend.

David would be Saul's target again and again as the king sent his men—and sometimes went himself—in search of the man he hoped to kill. Jonathan continued his faithful dedication.

> While David was at Horesh in the Desert of Ziph, he learned that Saul had come out to take his life. And Saul's son Jonathan went to David at Horesh and helped him find strength in God. "Don't be afraid," he said. "My father Saul will not lay a hand on you. You will be king over Israel, and I will be second to you. Even my father Saul knows this." The two of them made a covenant before the LORD. Then Jonathan went home, but David remained at Horesh.
> 1 Samuel 23:15–18

There were also multiple occasions on which David had the upper hand over Saul and easily could have killed him, but each time he refused to harm the man the Lord had once chosen king.

Ultimately, it was the Philistines who killed Jonathan. Saul was also killed after trying to take his own life, then asking another man to put him out of his misery. There was no celebration for David. Instead, he praised them in song and lamented their deaths.

> From the blood of the slain,
>   from the flesh of the mighty,
>   the bow of Jonathan did not turn back,
>   the sword of Saul did not return unsatisfied.
> Saul and Jonathan—
>   in life they were loved and admired,
>   and in death they were not parted.

They were swifter than eagles,
they were stronger than lions.
2 Samuel 1:22–23

The beauty of David's song reminds us how David had come to know Saul and Jonathan, as the young man who played music for Saul when he was deeply troubled. It was his musical gift that had brought David to Saul and Jonathan in the first place, and it was by his musical gift that David honored them in their passing. Only at the end of his lament did David speak of Jonathan his friend instead of Jonathan the prince, and those verses are among the most heartbreaking and beautiful in all of Scripture:

I grieve for you, Jonathan my brother;
    you were very dear to me.
Your love for me was wonderful,
    more wonderful than that of women.
How the mighty have fallen!
The weapons of war have perished!
2 Samuel 1:25–27

The word for love David used here is *ahavah* or *ahabah*. It's a powerful Hebrew word used to describe God's love toward us (Isaiah 43:4) and Abraham's love for his son Isaac (Genesis 22:3), among other occurrences in the Old Testament. David also paired it with the word "wonderful" as it's used in the context of God's miraculous, saving work. It's the word used to describe the *wonders* God would perform in striking down the Egyptians in Exodus 3:20. We see it again when Joshua foretells the *amazing things* God would do for His people, like parting the Jordan

River (Joshua 3:5). Think about that for a minute: David likened Jonathan's friendship to God's biggest miracles. He is the God who works wonders, including the treasured gift of a beloved friend.

Long after losing his devoted friend, Jonathan, and becoming king himself, David never forgot the pledge they'd made to each other. As king, David broke the norms of the day when he decided to honor the house of Saul—the man who had repeatedly tried to kill him. It was customary for new kings to wipe out the family and legacy of the king they were replacing. Instead, we see mercy and a tangible reminder of the enduring covenant of friendship between Jonathan and David.

> David asked, "Is there anyone still left of the house of Saul to whom I can show kindness for Jonathan's sake?"
> Now there was a servant of Saul's household named Ziba. They summoned him to appear before David, and the king said to him, "Are you Ziba?"
> "At your service," he replied.
> 2 Samuel 9:1–2

No one would have blamed Ziba for being apprehensive in response to King David's questions. As you'll soon see, Saul's associates and descendants had been in hiding following his death—probably for years. They'd been on the run, fully aware that the rules of that time could easily mean a death sentence for them.

But David would never betray the vow he'd made to Jonathan. In fact, he was looking to make good on his promises.

The king asked, "Is there no one still alive from the house of Saul to whom I can show God's kindness?"

Ziba answered the king, "There is still a son of Jonathan; he is lame in both feet."

"Where is he?" the king asked.

Ziba answered, "He is at the house of Makir son of Ammiel in Lo Debar."

2 Samuel 9:3–4

There are so many fascinating nuggets in this exchange. First, the story behind how Jonathan's son had come to be lame. We find the answer back in 2 Samuel 4, when the then five-year-old boy was suddenly taken on the run in the wake of his father and grandfather's deaths.

His nurse picked him up and fled, but as she hurried to leave, he fell and became disabled.

2 Samuel 4:4

And as close as David and Jonathan had been, it appears the king had no idea about this son of Jonathan's who was still alive. Jonathan's boy had once been the grandson of a king, and yet he'd been hiding out in someone else's house, under the care of Makir. If you jump forward a few chapters, you learn that Makir was a devoted supporter of King David at a time when he was fighting for his political and literal life (2 Samuel 17:27–29). Life for Mephibosheth was about to change.

David had Jonathan's son brought to the palace. What must he have thought when he was summoned? Did Mephibosheth

THE LOVE STORIES OF THE BIBLE SPEAK

know of the unbreakable bond between his father and the king? Had he also heard the stories about Saul trying to murder David? Whatever fears or questions Mephibosheth had as he approached David and bowed were quickly calmed.

> David said, "Mephibosheth!"
>
> "At your service," he replied.
>
> "Don't be afraid," David said to him, "for I will surely show you kindness for the sake of your father Jonathan. I will restore to you all the land that belonged to your grandfather Saul, and you will always eat at my table."
>
> Mephibosheth bowed down and said, "What is your servant, that you should notice a dead dog like me?"
>
> 2 Samuel 9:6b–8

David not only embraced Mephibosheth, but he restored him. The king not only gave Jonathan's son all the land that belonged to Saul, but in the verses that follow we also see David assigning servants to work that land so that it would bring great benefit to Mephibosheth. And, yes, Mephibosheth joined King David's table, being treated like one of the royal sons. The covenant of David and Jonathan's friendship lasted a lifetime.

We live in a world that is constantly telling us romantic love is the highest ideal, often suggesting that other relationships like friendships are somehow lesser. Just look at the magazine racks in the bookstore to see how many are dedicated to brides and marriage. There's a booming "wedding industry," but what about a "friendship industry"? Laugh if you must, but I could get behind something like that! To put someone in the "friend zone" is viewed as a negative, but think about what our culture is missing by suggesting that romance is the only valuable way to connect with someone.

My friends are a true joy and treasure in my life. Together, we've cheered each other's successes and grieved crushing losses. We've had each other's backs when one of us is under attack. We've shared secrets, hopes, dreams and locked lots of conversations tightly within "the cone of silence." My life is infinitely richer because of these confidants and cheerleaders. I cannot imagine the void that would exist in my heart and my life without them. In giving us the example of David and Jonathan, the Bible calls to honor the love of friendship. The Bible beckons us to recognize the wonder, the miracle that is true, covenanted friendship-love.

Prayer: Lord, You bless us with the miracle of friendship. Help us to remember to cherish and celebrate it! Please open our hearts and our minds to the connection of companionship. Just as You are our Faithful Friend, may we learn to be a steady confidant to others. Spur us always to put You and Your wondrous love at the center of our friendships.

SHADRACH, MESHACH, AND ABEDNEGO

Friendship in the Fire

Daniel 1–3, Psalm 137, Jeremiah 29:1–11

This story has always inspired and challenged me, and it reminds me of the power of community and friendships in the midst of life's fiercest storms. In the book of Daniel, we meet a group of friends thrown into a terrifying situation that would test everything about their lives and their faith. Stripped away from their families and their homes, the men had God and each other. I have no doubt He put them together to stand as a band of brave witnesses, willing to face even death in order to honor God. What a treasure God gives us when He blesses us with courageous brothers and sisters committed to standing in unity when trials come.

The book of Daniel unfolds in the wake of King Nebuchadnezzar of Babylon laying siege to Jerusalem. This would happen more than once. Nebuchadnezzar conquered Israel in three separate attacks. Nebuchadnezzar first invaded Jerusalem in 605 BC, and would go on to attack Jerusalem twice more, taking thousands of Israelites captive. He finally destroyed the temple and left Jerusalem in ruins after his final siege in 586 BC. These invasions by Babylon were traumatic for God's people. Not only were they forcibly separated from their homeland, but the temple in Jerusalem—the Jews' central place for worship, representing God's presence among His people—was eventually demolished. It must have felt like God had abandoned them.

Psalm 137 expresses the desolation the Jewish people experienced at this event, and it is a haunting description of grief:

> By the rivers of Babylon we sat and wept
> when we remembered Zion.
> There on the poplars
> we hung our harps,
> for there our captors asked us for songs,
> our tormentors demanded songs of joy;
> they said, "Sing us one of the songs of Zion!"
> How can we sing the songs of the LORD
> while in a foreign land?
> If I forget you, Jerusalem,
> may my right hand forget its skill.
> May my tongue cling to the roof of my mouth
> if I do not remember you,
> if I do not consider Jerusalem
> my highest joy.
>   Psalm 137:1-6

During this period of the Babylonian exile the Jewish people were forced to find new ways to connect to their faith in a world where there was no more temple, no more land of promise. They still had the words of God, and those took on new importance during the seventy years they were exiled in Babylon. It would be decades before they would return home, to the cherished traditions and security they had once known.

The Jewish exiles who eventually returned to Jerusalem took with them stories of their time in Babylon—narratives of the heroes and teachers of the faith who had sustained them during that heartbreaking time of trials. God had not been absent from His people during those years. He had spoken powerfully to the prophet Ezekiel, who had foreseen a day when the "dry bones" of the house of Israel would rise again and become a new, resurrected people. God had spoken to Daniel the prophet, and He had rescued Daniel's three friends—Shadrach, Meshach, and Abednego—from an execution order at the hands of Nebuchadnezzar in a victory for the God of Israel that His people would never forget.

And while every story and song I've ever heard about the trio uses those names, the men never called themselves Shadrach, Meshach, and Abednego. They were Jews who bore proudly their Jewish names: Hananiah, Mishael, and Azariah. Hananiah means "the grace of God," Azariah means "the help of God," and Mishael means "who is like the Mighty One?" These young men were given Babylonian names when they were taken from their homes and forcibly entered into the king's service. Part of Nebuchadnezzar's plan to subjugate the people of Israel was to keep them from teaching Jewish language, culture, and religion to their young people. After Nebuchadnezzar attacked Israel and took some of the articles from the temple back to Babylon, he ordered some of the Israelites themselves to be carried off as well.

Then the king ordered Ashpenaz, chief of his court officials, to bring into the king's service some of the Israelites

from the royal family and the nobility—young men without any physical defect, handsome, showing aptitude for every kind of learning, well informed, quick to understand, and qualified to serve in the king's palace.
Daniel 1:3–4a

There was a method to the king's madness. Israel's finest, having been uprooted and carried to a foreign land, were to be immersed in the Babylonian language and literature. They were also assigned a daily portion of food and wine from the king's table, something that would have been highly elevated beyond what the average person would have had access to. Daniel 1:5 tells us the men were to undergo three full years of training and then be assigned to the king's service. In an effort to break their identities and reshape them into loyal subjects, the men were given those new names: Shadrach for Hananiah, Meshach for Mishael, and Abednego for Azariah. Daniel was also given a new name—Belteshazzar—which Nebuchadnezzar described in Daniel 4:8 as "after the name of my god."

Notice the three things that the royal training zeroed in on: language, literature, and food. Everything that made them distinctly Jewish would be replaced. They would no longer speak Hebrew—which probably meant no praying in Hebrew and no conversing with other Jews in Hebrew. They would learn Babylonian literature, which likely meant they would not have as much time to read Scripture. Lastly, they would eat and drink only what the king assigned to them. That may sound inconvenient and strange to us, but it was strikingly more important than that in this context. For the Jewish people food was—and is—one of the main ways they obeyed God's commands, by following the kosher dietary laws laid down in the book of Leviticus and elsewhere. That meant they could eat only meat and wine prepared in a certain way, and definitely not any that had been offered to–or arguably "blessed"–by foreign gods. By denying these young men kosher food, the Babylonians were denying them the ability to worship and obey God as He had commanded them.

Isn't this just like something the enemy tries to do in our hearts and minds today? Even if–maybe, especially if–you've been raised to know the Bible and walk with God, the enemy will try to dull your senses and sidetrack your heart. Yes, we are to live in the world. That's where we shine God's light and work to grow His kingdom. It's where we meet people in our neighborhoods, schools, workplaces, and even the grocery store–in order to share the good news of God's unconditional love for every one of them. The enemy loves to distract us with worldly temptations, and they don't even have to be bad things! But by drawing us away from the foundations and tenets of our faith and tempting us to replace them with modern ideas and comforts, he tries to give us a new name and bury what we know to be the truth. Nebuchadnezzar aimed to do the same to Daniel and his friends.

Daniel was unafraid to stand his ground.

But Daniel resolved not to defile himself with the royal food and wine, and he asked the chief official for permission not to defile himself this way.
   Daniel 1:8

Notice that before Daniel ever asked permission to deviate from the king's commands, he had already decided not to cave.

And he wasn't alone. What an incredible gift of God's grace that three of Daniel's friends would stand strong with him. That wasn't God's only divine provision for Daniel. Just one verse later we learn, "God had caused the official to show favor and compassion to Daniel." (Daniel 1:9) Even still, that man worried about what would happen to him if Daniel and his buddies showed up looking like they were falling apart. He worried "the king would then have my head" if they appeared unfit and in worse shape than the others.

So Daniel proposed a test for ten days to show the official he and his devout friends would not suffer because of their diet consisting of nothing but vegetables and water. God honored their faithfulness.

> At the end of the ten days they looked healthier and better nourished than any of the young men who ate the royal food. So the guard took away their choice food and the wine they were to drink and gave them vegetables instead. To these four young men God gave knowledge and understanding of all kinds of literature and learning. And Daniel could understand visions and dreams of all kinds.
> Daniel 1:15–17

What was essentially "civil disobedience" by this courageous quartet paid off, and it's worth our time and attention to notice the *way* in which they resisted. These young men couldn't change the reality and limitations of their circumstances as Babylonian captives. But they could change the way in which they lived under those circumstances. There is a real lesson for us here. Sometimes we can't escape where we are in life, but we can choose how we respond and navigate the situation. We can hold tight to our faith and our calling, even when we can do nothing about the world around us. That may mean denying ourselves. Shadrach, Meshach, and Abednego surely must have missed the taste of meat and wine, but they knew it was far better to obey God's commands than give in to the seductive luxuries of Babylon.

Notice, too, the supernatural abilities God bestowed on these valiant young men. It wasn't the Babylonians who gave them knowledge and understanding—it was God who granted them those skills. God rewarded their sacrifice, and it brought Him glory.

> At the end of the time set by the king to bring them into his service, the chief official presented them to Nebuchadnezzar. The king talked with them, and he found none equal to Daniel, Hananiah, Mishael and Azariah; so they entered the king's service. In every matter of wisdom and understanding about which the king questioned them, he found them ten times better than all the magicians and enchanters in his whole kingdom.
>
> Daniel 1:18–20

Ten times better! It was no contest. The four young friends had become magi—wise men in the Babylonian court. They never abandoned their faith, and God didn't ask them to abandon their secular calling either. He placed them in a lofty place and gave them the gifts they needed in order to serve Him there.

Friendships create community, and what a source of strength

that is. I know it's something I missed terribly during the extended period our churches in the Washington, DC, area were ordered to close during the pandemic. I missed singing together, praying over each other, and seeing my girlfriends and their families. I'm sure many of you reading this book experienced the pain of isolation. It was unnerving and reminded me how much we are designed to rely on each other.

What a blessing that Daniel and his friends had the privilege of standing together in the face of having the foundations of their lives ripped out from underneath them. Together, Daniel and his three friends presented a united front to the royal officials and created a coalition of their own. Far from the Holy Land and far from the temple, the men remained near to God. This is one of the special blessings of friendship: It can create a place for our faith to flourish even when the outside world is against us. Godly friends remind us who we are—and *Whose* we are—even when the world tempts us to forget.

Times of Trial

Daniel, Shadrach, Meshach, and Abednego were vaulted within the kingdom, but that also opened them up to danger when the king became enraged over something they had no earthly ability to control. It was a dream that troubled Nebuchadnezzar, but rather than tell his "magicians, enchanters, sorcerers and astrologers" what it was, the king demanded that *they* tell *him* what he'd dreamed. They argued that no man would be capable of doing that. He responded by telling them he would cut them "into pieces" and have their houses "turned into piles of rubble." (Daniel 2:5) In those days, dream interpretation was a central part of the job of the king's wise men or magi. When pressed again by the king, they repeated their argument that no one could possibly know what the king had dreamed.

> This made the king so angry and furious that he ordered the execution of all the wise men of Babylon. So the decree was issued to put the wise men to death, and men were sent to look for Daniel and his friends to put them to death.
> Daniel 2:12–13

The king's fury meant even the people he'd once praised as being "ten times" better than all his other wise men were being caught up in his execution order.

When the commander of Nebuchadnezzar's army went to carry out the death warrants, we're told that "Daniel spoke to him with wisdom and tact." (Daniel 2:14b) Daniel was able to go directly to the king to discuss the dream then returned home to strategize with his friends, the loyal band of confidants bound together by their faith.

> Then Daniel returned to his house and explained the matter to his friends Hananiah, Mishael and Azariah. He urged them to plead for mercy from the God of heaven concerning this mystery, so that he and his friends might not be executed with the rest of the wise men of Babylon.

> During the night the mystery was revealed to Daniel in a
> vision.
>   Daniel 2:17–19

I love that this passage shows us Daniel and his friends were still using their original Jewish names to address each other. Regardless of the attempts to strip them of their religious and cultural pride and identity, they supported each other in staying true to who they really were.

These friends also joined together in fervent prayer for God's mercy and discernment. Christ highlighted the power of praying friends meeting together in Matthew 18:

> For where two or three gather in my name, there am I with
> them.
>   Matthew 18:20

When Daniel was up against the toughest challenge of his life—perhaps with only hours of that life left—he knew the wisest thing to do was to share that burden with his brothers in faith. It was a prudent move. God honored their shared prayers and revealed all that Daniel needed to know.

Daniel didn't take credit, or even give it to his faithful friends. He directed all praise to God.

> Praise be to the name of God for ever and ever;
>   wisdom and power are his.
>   He changes times and seasons;
>   he deposes kings and raises up others.
>   He gives wisdom to the wise

and knowledge to the discerning.
He reveals deep and hidden things;
he knows what lies in darkness,
and light dwells with him.
I thank and praise you, God of my ancestors:
You have given me wisdom and power,
you have made known to me what we asked of you,
you have made known to us the dream of the king.
Daniel 2:20–23

Note his words of thanks to God for what "we asked of you" and "you have made known to us." *We* and *us*. These friends were in it together. None of them was left standing alone in the face of an almost-certain death sentence.

Daniel was able to go to the king and both tell him about the dream itself and then interpret it. Nebuchadnezzar was so impressed that he "fell prostrate" before Daniel "and paid him honor." (Daniel 2:46) And that wasn't all.

The king said to Daniel, "Surely your God is the God of gods and the Lord of kings and a revealer of mysteries, for you were able to reveal this mystery."

Then the king placed Daniel in a high position and lavished many gifts on him. He made him ruler over the entire province of Babylon and placed him in charge of all its wise men. Moreover, at Daniel's request the king appointed Shadrach, Meshach and Abednego administrators over the province of Babylon, while Daniel himself remained at the royal court.

Daniel 2:47–49

These devoted friends stuck together time and again when their very lives were in danger. Together they committed to God's principles. They had prayed together and had been honored by both God and man. Yet, despite their successes and new positions, their biggest test was still to come.

Royal memories are short, and the favor the king had extended to the young men was conditioned on their loyalty to the king above all else. That was a condition these young Jewish men would never accept because their commitment was to the God of Israel over everything else. And when King Nebuchadnezzar decided to create a giant idol and demanded that everyone immediately bow down and worship the image as soon as they heard music playing—the esteemed friends had a choice to make. Nebuchadnezzar didn't offer an out.

Whoever does not fall down and worship will immediately be thrown into a blazing furnace.
Daniel 3:6

This wasn't just any idol—it was a statue made of gold, some sixty cubits high and six cubits wide, or ninety feet high and nine feet wide. That's no statue but a colossus! Everyone understood they were to stop at once, fall down and pray to this idol as soon as the music started.

Guess who took a hard pass? You got it. And some of the king's advisers saw the perfect opportunity to take out the honorable young men the king himself had praised and exalted: Shadrach, Meshach, and Abednego.

They started by lavishly praising the king and appealing to his pride, carefully emphasizing exactly what he'd ordered everyone to do. Then they dropped the bomb: *There are people defying you, king!*

> . . . there are some Jews whom you have set over the affairs of the province of Babylon—Shadrach, Meshach and Abednego—who pay no attention to you, Your Majesty. They neither serve your gods nor worship the image of gold you have set up.
> Daniel 3:12

Predictably, the king was furious. He summoned the three friends—who had been trusted enough to occupy high political positions in his government—and demanded to know if the accusation was true. He threatened them with death unless they complied with his order:

> But if you do not worship it, you will be thrown immediately into a blazing furnace. Then what god will be able to rescue you from my hand?
> Daniel 3:15

Whether he knew it or not, Nebuchanezzar had just teed up the perfect opportunity for these brave friends to clearly articulate what they were all about.

> Shadrach, Meshach and Abednego replied to him, "King Nebuchadnezzar, we do not need to defend ourselves before you in this matter. If we are thrown into the blazing furnace, the God we serve is able to deliver us from it, and he will deliver us from Your Majesty's hand. But even if

he does not, we want you to know, Your Majesty, that we will not serve your gods or worship the image of gold you have set up."

Daniel 3:16–18

This speech makes me want to pump my fist in the air and yell, "Hallelujah!" If you ever need a shot of courage, read over these words a few times.

This trio made it clear they knew that God, the God of Israel, was fully capable of sparing them from the flames that could easily destroy their human bodies. But they also let the king know that *even if* God chose not to perform that miracle, there was absolutely zero chance they'd cave. Think about that for a minute. The friends acknowledged that God's *power* was infinite but that His *will* was unknowable. God could absolutely save them, but it might not be His will to do so—and that was okay.

We have all had moments in life when we were forced to accept this reality. I struggled with this as a Christian for a long time. I will often pray that God would heal a loved one or untangle a disastrous situation, but I've learned that my heart also has to be willing to accept His decision. That doesn't make my prayers any less important. We see many times in the Bible where God hears the prayers of His people and responds with compassion. What we are called to do is to be trusting and selfless enough to do what Shadrach, Meshach, and Abednego did here before the king: proclaim God's unparalleled power to act and humble ourselves to His ultimate decision.

These friends were bound together in their faith and in their unwavering commitment to each other. Not one of them peeled off and said, "Okay, king, I'm not with those guys. I'd like to live." The Bible provides us this concrete example of the power we find in community, in sticking together with trusted companions when the very worst happens in our lives. They stood together. They spoke together. And they were willing to die together. They told the king, with extraordinary calm, that they didn't need to defend themselves to him—and wouldn't.

Given their history, it must have been tempting to shout at the king, "You have already seen the miracles that the God of Israel can do!" They may have wanted to accuse the king of injustice, irrational anger, or despotic cruelty—and they would have been right. But they didn't do any of that. Instead, they kept the focus of their speech on God alone. Their friendship strengthened them enough to make this bold statement of faith.

Our friendships can be a great source of accountability and spiritual growth.

> As iron sharpens iron,
>   so one person sharpens another.
> Proverbs 27:17

Who in your life offers accountability and wisdom? Do you provide that to others in your sphere? These friends, uprooted and forced into the service of their oppressor, spent years having each other's backs. The persecution had started in small ways, and they remained united. By the time it literally turned into a life-and-death situation, they had the courage to stand together. That doesn't happen overnight. It takes an investment of time, transparency, and vulnerability to form meaningful bonds. It takes showing up when things are dicey. These friends weren't just unified when they were promoted and praised. They were rock solid when faced with death itself.

Triumph and Revelation

Following their courageous speech, the king was "furious." (Daniel 3:19) We're told "his attitude toward them had changed." I bet! In a blinding rage, the king demanded that the furnace be heated seven times hotter than usual. He then ordered his soldiers to bind the friends and throw them into the furnace fully clothed. The backdraft from the furnace was so intense that it killed the men who carried out the king's orders.

In the normal course of events, Shadrach, Meshach, and Abednego would have been dead within seconds. But there was nothing "normal" about what happened next.

> Then King Nebuchadnezzar leaped to his feet in amazement and asked his advisers, "Weren't there three men that we tied up and threw into the fire?" They replied, "Certainly, Your Majesty." He said, "Look! I see four men walking around in the fire, unbound and unharmed, and the fourth looks like a son of the gods." Nebuchadnezzar then approached the opening of the blazing furnace and shouted, "Shadrach, Meshach and Abednego, servants of the Most High God, come out! Come here!" So Shadrach, Meshach and Abednego came out of the fire, and the satraps, prefects, governors and royal advisers crowded

around them. They saw that the fire had not harmed their bodies, nor was a hair of their heads singed; their robes were not scorched, and there was no smell of fire on them.

Daniel 3:24–27

God not only saved His three faithful servants, but He also showed King Nebuchadnezzar powerful visual witness to the reality of the true Lord of heaven and earth—the sight of an angel of God, many scholars believe it was Jesus Himself, protecting and guarding Shadrach, Meshach, and Abednego in the midst of a deadly inferno.

Nebuchadnezzar was astounded, and he immediately offered praise to God—the God of Israel. He also praised the three friends for their faithfulness to their God, even at the risk of their own lives:

They trusted in him and defied the king's command and were willing to give up their lives rather than serve or worship any god except their own God.

Daniel 3:28

That was exactly the kind of loyalty Nebuchadnezzar wanted for himself, but this astonishing miracle gave him a wake-up call. How could the king ever expect these Jewish young men to bow to a mere human or lifeless idol when their God was capable of this! Nebuchadnezzar never pledged his heart and life to God, but he saw and acknowledged the power of something—Someone—who was greater than he was. He saw that true faith could not be manipulated for political purposes, even under the threat of execution.

Throughout the centuries, Christians have seen in the story of Shadrach, Meshach, and Abednego more than just an adventure with a dramatic ending. Some of the oldest Christian art in the world depicts Shadrach, Meshach, and Abednego in the fiery furnace. In the Catacombs of Priscilla in Rome there is a fresco that shows the three friends walking in the midst of the fire, their arms raised in prayer. Why would this obscure biblical story have spoken with such power to the early Christians?

For Christians in the Roman Empire who endured regular persecution and who had seen members of their own communities—and maybe their own family members—suffer torture and death for their faith, these three friends would have given them courage to face the Nebuchadnezzar of their own time. They knew they were not the first to face persecution for their belief in the God of Israel. And like Shadrach, Meshach, and Abednego, they knew their lives were in God's hands. They held fast to the story of these three friends whose faith had turned aside the fires of hell itself and whose love for God sustained them. They cherished the story in part because it was the men's friendship—their community of believers—that had given them the strength to endure.

Those early Christians also lived lives that made them seem strange to those around them—just like the three friends in the Babylonian court. But those tight-knit Christian communities held together. Shadrach, Meshach, and Abednego modeled friendship, and the faith that grew stronger when it was shared. Ancient Christians hiding in the catacombs looked at that image of the three friends and saw themselves: a beautiful reflection of the love of God that mirrored the brotherhood of Christian love.

The story is also one of great inspiration for modern-day Christians living through persecution. Most of us won't face the same kinds of threats, but any Christian who follows Jesus' commands will face hardship. That's clear.

> In fact, everyone who wants to live a godly life in Christ Jesus will be persecuted.
> 2 Timothy 3:12

> I have told you these things, so that in me you may have peace. In this world you will have trouble. But take heart! I have overcome the world.
> John 16:33

Whether we are mocked for our faith or face more grave dangers, we can be tempted to withdraw from the world around us. The story of the Babylonian exiles reminds us why we should resist that impulse. In rare cases, withdrawal may be a Christian's calling, but look at Jesus. He spent most of his life engaging with the world, even amid growing threats. It's a good thing for us that He did! We should do likewise.

God wants us to engage in His creation, find ways we can use our skills within it, and flourish. Jesus prayed to His father for His followers, who were hated "for they are not of the world . . . My prayer is not that you take them out of the world but that you protect them from the evil one." (John 17:14–15) He wanted us to be in the world, but not *of* it. Daniel and his friends showed us how to do that.

As the people of Israel struggled with exile, the prophet Jeremiah gave them this message from God.

> "Build houses and settle down; plant gardens and eat what they produce. . . . Seek the peace and prosperity of the city

to which I have carried you into exile. Pray to the LORD for it, because if it prospers, you too will prosper. . . . When seventy years are completed for Babylon, I will come to you and fulfill my good promise to bring you back to this place. For I know the plans I have for you," declares the LORD, "plans to prosper you and not to harm you, plans to give you hope and a future."

Jeremiah 29:5-11

You've likely heard that last verse, maybe without knowing the full context. It's important to remember it was a message from God to people who would never return to their homeland. It's a message of hope, but not a promise of immediate deliverance. It was a promise that God would bless them in exile, and that there was always hope because God was working out His plan for their future.

I hope those words encourage you the same way they reassure me. God is with us, even in Babylon. He can use us here to bring grace to the world around us. He can change the hearts of pagan kings. He can walk with us into the furnace. He can and does bless us with a community of believers. And one day He will take us home to our heavenly Promised Land.

Prayer: Almighty God, help us to support our brothers and sisters when life is good and when it is trying. Spur us to be vulnerable and transparent so that we may find strength in our unity. May we sharpen and challenge each other to grow in our knowledge of—and commitment to—You. Guide us to inspire and embolden each other to stand in the face of trouble.

Companions for the Journey

After many moves over the years, personal and professional, I recently went through a box of things from my college and law school days and found the Bible I'd gotten as a teenager. Among other things, it contained a pass to a Steven Curtis Chapman concert amid the dog-eared and underlined passages marked with lots of different colors of ink. It's also got my maiden name embossed right there on the front. I have so many memories of taking that Bible all over the world with me, sometimes crying my eyes out and looking for God's answers. Other times I simply soaked in the promises of His guidance and protection. I love that it has all those colorful maps from ancient times, showing the various paths of Jesus' ministry and Paul's (whom we first meet as Saul) missionary trips. There's something about visualizing the real-world places they traveled that makes those journeys come to life.

Paul's trips crisscrossing those maps are fascinating. He crossed oceans and traveled all over the Mediterranean. Those maps represent a hero's journey of adventure through peril and hardship. I often pictured Paul as a solo traveler, overcoming against all odds, armed with his faith alone, bravely facing beatings, imprisonments, and shipwreck. But the reality is, throughout his ministry, Paul was sustained by friends and companions who made those missionary journeys possible. Each was a joint venture, undertaken by Paul along with at least one other friend. Those dotted lines weaving across the map of the Mediterranean are the reason you and I are Christians today. Paul had trusted colleagues and friends working alongside him, and multiple churches that supported him with prayer and resources. Early Christianity was built on a network of believers, and friendship was the engine of the early Church.

Just as we saw with David and Jonathan, and Shadrach, Meshach, and Abednego—friendships infuse us with courage and blanket us in love. They can be a powerful source of help and encouragement and equip us for the tasks God has designed for us. They are also a reminder of His great provision and love for us. The Lord knew Paul would need all kinds of friends in order to carry out his ministry, including from the very moment he came to see God's truth. Paul's life and teachings offer us not only deep theological truths but also lessons on the importance and gift of community.

Ananias (Acts 9:1–19)

One of the first friends we see upon Saul's conversion didn't exactly want to make his acquaintance. That's because Saul was there when Stephen was stoned "giving approval to his death,"

(Acts 8:1) and he'd made it his mission to destroy the young church of Jesus followers. When we catch up with Saul just one chapter later he was busy "breathing out murderous threats" against the disciples (Acts 9:1). He'd even gone to the high priest and asked for letters giving him permission to drag any Christ followers he found in Damascus back to Jerusalem as prisoners. Saul was a bad dude.

It was on that trip to Damascus that Saul got his wake-up call.

As he neared Damascus on his journey, suddenly a light from heaven flashed around him. He fell to the ground and heard a voice say to him, "Saul, Saul, why do you persecute me?"

"Who are you, LORD?" Saul asked.

"I am Jesus, whom you are persecuting," he replied. "Now get up and go into the city, and you will be told what you must do."

The men traveling with Saul stood there speechless; they heard the sound but did not see anyone. Saul got up from the ground, but when he opened his eyes he could see nothing. So they led him by the hand into Damascus. For three days he was blind, and did not eat or drink anything.

Acts 9:3–9

Talk about getting someone's attention! Saul had been hit with the power and presence of Jesus Christ. There was no denying this radical reality check.

The Lord reached out to a believer named Ananias there in

Damascus and told him to go to Saul. I think we can all understand why he didn't want to!

> "LORD," Ananias answered, "I have heard many reports about this man and all the harm he has done to your holy people in Jerusalem. And he has come here with authority from the chief priests to arrest all who call on your name."
> Acts 9:13

Forget all that, the Lord said. He not only wanted Ananias to go minister to Saul, but that onetime hunter of Christians was about to become one of Christ's most powerful and prolific evangelizers.

> But the LORD said to Ananias, "Go! This man is my chosen instrument to proclaim my name to the Gentiles and their kings and to the people of Israel."
> Acts 9:15

Ananias obeyed the Lord and went to Saul, despite his fears. Imagine the phony conversions the early Christians had to fear, someone infiltrating their homes and churches with the sole purpose of harming them. Ananias trusted the Lord and went to the stricken man once hellbent on killing people just like him. He told Saul he'd been sent by the Lord "so that you may see again and be filled with the Holy Spirit." (Acts 9:17) That's exactly what happened. Saul regained his physical sight, and his spiritual blindness fell away too. I think it's fair to say Ananias was Saul's first Christian friend, and certainly one God sent to help Saul launch his wide-reaching mission to spread the Gospel.

Barnabas (Acts 9:26–30, 11:19–30, 15:1–12)

Immediately after his conversion, Saul astonished people by beginning to teach in the synagogues of Damascus that Jesus Christ was the Son of God.

> Saul grew more and more powerful and baffled the Jews living in Damascus by proving that Jesus is the Messiah.
> Acts 9:22

Imagine the shock of someone who had been a murderous oppressor of anyone who worshipped Christ preaching that very thing! Saul so offended the Jews in Damascus that they wanted to kill him. Talk about going from hunter to hunted. He was snuck safely out of the city, and in Galatians 1 we learn he spent years in other regions before he went to Jerusalem and "tried to join the disciples." (Acts 9:26) That's where we first hear about his relationship with Barnabas.

But first, who was Barnabas? He initially appears in the early chapters of the book of Acts:

> Joseph, a Levite from Cyprus, whom the apostles called Barnabas (which means "son of encouragement") sold a field he owned and brought the money and put it at the apostles' feet.
> Acts 4:36

We know that Barnabas was a Jewish believer, and was evidently well-known to the disciples. He was probably a man of some means, given that he had property he was able to sell to use to fund the Christian community in Jerusalem. His name hints that he was a trusted encourager, in addition to his financial support.

So, Barnabas was a key ally when Saul showed up in Jerusalem. The disciples were "all afraid" of Saul and "not believing that he really was a disciple." (Acts 9:26) Though Saul had been a Christian for some period of time, they evidently hadn't been convinced.

> But Barnabas took him and brought him to the apostles. He told them how Saul on his journey had seen the LORD and that the LORD had spoken to him, and how in Damascus he had preached fearlessly in the name of Jesus. So Saul stayed with them and moved about freely in Jerusalem, speaking boldly in the name of the LORD.
> Acts 9:27–28

Barnabas was clearly liked and trusted by both Saul and the apostles, and his friendship with the once-lethal persecutor was solid enough to serve as a bridge between the two.

We all need friends who will advocate for us, to vouch for us in the face of doubters. And we need to be that kind of friend too. Are you willing to spend some of your social capital in order to make sure an unknown companion gets a fair shake in an unfamiliar situation? I've got an interesting network of girlfriends in the Washington, DC, area. When one of us brings someone new to a dinner or an event, they already have the seal of approval. We trust each other to invite in a new woman only if she's truly drama-free and knows how to keep a secret! Over the years I've been that woman, and I've also been the one bringing in that

unfamiliar face. I have faith in my friends that if they have confidence in someone, I will too. That's exactly what Saul needed—
and had—in Barnabas. Barnabas' intercession had the desired
result: The apostles accepted Saul (though maybe warily). Saul
would later write that he stayed with Peter for fifteen days and
saw none of the other apostles except James, Jesus' brother (Galatians 1:18–19).

During these years, as believers were persecuted, many of
them scattered. They took the good news of the Gospel with them.
Some were only spreading the message of Christ with other Jews,
while others were reaching out to Gentiles as well—including in
Antioch. When the apostles in Jerusalem heard about the evan-
gelism in Antioch, they sent Barnabas there, the very first Christian to go on a missionary journey. Barnabas was delighted with
what he found.

> When he arrived and saw what the grace of God had done,
> he was glad and encouraged them all to remain true to
> the LORD with all their hearts. He was a good man, full of
> the Holy Spirit and faith, and a great number of people
> were brought to the LORD. Then Barnabas went to Tar-
> sus to look for Saul, and when he found him, he brought
> him to Antioch. So for a whole year Barnabas and Saul met
> with the church and taught great numbers of people. The
> disciples were called Christians first at Antioch.
> Acts 11:23–26

There is so much beautiful Christian history packed into this
brief passage! We get a firsthand look at that encouraging spirit
Barnabas had, and see that he took the initiative to get Saul from

Tarsus to help him in the work of the Gospel. Barnabas knew that his friend had great gifts to share with the church around the world. For a year they spread the good news of Jesus with scores of people in Antioch.

Barnabas knew Saul had a unique calling. As the "son of encouragement," Barnabas made it his task to cultivate and honor those talents in his friend, even if it meant he had to track him down to do it! That also signals to us that Barnabas did not have the kind of pride that could get in the way of God's mission. There was nothing in him that said, *Well, this is MY mission, I don't want to share it with anyone else!* He had a clear-headed picture of his own gifts and strengths, and he knew that Saul's talents were needed too. So successful was the formation of Christian identity that Saul and Barnabas forged together in Antioch that you and I are called "Christians" today because of the work they did there.

The best kinds of friends will always be cheering for each other's successes. I have girlfriends who travel the world in ministry, write books, or pour into their children 24/7. It makes my day when they send updates on their triumphs. Just this week I got a video from a friend whose little son quoted an incredibly long passage of Scripture from memory. He'd worked so hard on that, and I knew his Mama had coached him for weeks. Bravo! Another friend had a book hit *The New York Times* bestseller list yesterday. Excellent! Yet another won a seat on her town's school board. Awesome! There's no reason to be threatened by someone else's success. God has given each of us specific gifts and assignments. Barnabas knew and embraced that.

While Barnabas and Saul were serving together in Antioch,

many other prophets and teachers also rose up in the ministry. They realized it was time for the duo to take their preaching on the road.

> While they were worshiping the LORD and fasting, the Holy Spirit said, "Set apart for me Barnabas and Saul for the work to which I have called them." So after they had fasted and prayed, they placed their hands on them and sent them off.
> Acts 13:2–3

This time, the friends embarked on a sea voyage to Barnabas' home island of Cyprus. God had plans for them, and Saul was always aware of the assignment.

> For we are God's handiwork, created in Christ Jesus to do good works, which God prepared in advance for us to do.
> Ephesians 2:10

This first wide-ranging journey the two friends undertook went from Cyprus to Asia Minor—from Perga, to Pisidian Antioch, to Iconium, to Lystra and Derbe, and finally back to Antioch in Syria. From the beginning of this work we see their enemies plotting against them. One false prophet tried to sabotage their message to a leader who wanted to hear their message and had summoned them (Acts 13:9). Saul, filled with the Holy Spirit, called him out as "an enemy of everything that is right" and told him he'd lose his sight for a time. It happened immediately, which convinced the leader who'd asked them to come that Saul and his God were the real deal. Rather than being turned away from Christ, that leader embraced him and believed! (Acts 13:12)

It's during this time that we see Saul begin to be referred to as Paul. It wasn't uncommon in those days for people to have more than one name, alternately used based on the cultural space they were in at a particular time. Scholars say Saul was his Jewish given name, with Paul as the Latin option.

On one of their journeys, the friends were asked to share a message of encouragement at a particular synagogue. Paul asked his "Fellow Israelites and Gentiles who worship God" to listen as he gave a powerful sermon about God's grace and forgiveness through Jesus' sacrifice. The people were so moved that the two were invited back to speak again the following week. But some of the Jewish people were offended and "jealous" at the crowds Barnabas and Paul were attracting.

> But the Jewish leaders incited the God-fearing women of high standing and the leading men of the city. They stirred up persecution against Paul and Barnabas, and expelled them from their region. So they shook the dust off their feet as a warning to them and went to Iconium.
> Acts 13:50-51

The friends, committed to God and to each other in ministry, stayed united and moved forward.

Together, these godly companions faced all kinds of dangers and resistance. One time when Paul was stoned after their compelling teaching, the two simply traveled to a new city and kept sharing God's message of hope and redemption. Finally, after spreading the Gospel to Jews and Gentiles who would receive it, they went back to Antioch and shared all the exciting developments. And while Scripture tells us they stayed there "a long time," (Acts 14:28) it wasn't all drama-free.

Barnabas and Paul not only supported each other throughout their missionary journeys, but also back in Antioch when trouble started to bubble up. When some Jewish Christians came from Judea and told the Christians of Antioch that they needed to be circumcised and obey all the strictures of the Mosaic law, Paul and Barnabas pushed back—hard.

Certain people came down from Judea to Antioch and were teaching the believers: "Unless you are circumcised, according to the custom taught by Moses, you cannot be saved." This brought Paul and Barnabas into sharp dispute and debate with them. So Paul and Barnabas were appointed, along with some other believers, to go up to Jerusalem to see the apostles and elders about this question. The church sent them on their way, and as they traveled through Phoenicia and Samaria, they told how the Gentiles had been converted. This news made all the believers very glad. When they came to Jerusalem, they were welcomed by the church and the apostles and elders, to whom they reported everything God had done through them.

Acts 15:1-4

Barnabas and Paul stood shoulder to shoulder, defending the work they had begun throughout Syria, Asia Minor, and Cyprus. This was a brotherhood forged in the caldron of testing and trials. These friends were linked together by God and served as an enormous source of strength for one another.

This dispute over doctrine came to be called the Council of Jerusalem. On one side, Paul and Barnabas, and every other Jewish Christ-follower on the other side. Understandably, the other Jewish believers could not see how the redemption of Christ made any sense apart from God's saving work in the Jewish people. The message of the Gospel and the message of the Law were two parts of the whole, for them, and it must have been hard to understand how Paul and Barnabas could preach one but not the other. How could Jesus (grace) make any sense apart from his Jewish context (the law)?

With authority, Peter stood up to advocate for Paul and Barnabas, and it's clear his voice carried so much weight with the believers gathered there that it created space for the two men to speak.

> **The whole assembly became silent as they listened to Barnabas and Paul telling about the signs and wonders God had done among the Gentiles through them.**
>   Acts 15:12

Barnabas and Paul, because of the support they gave each other, weathered the storm of the Council of Jerusalem.

> **After spending some time there, they were sent off by the believers with the blessing of peace to return to those who had sent them. But Paul and Barnabas remained in Antioch, where they and many others taught and preached the word of the LORD.**
>   Acts 15:33–35

But like any real friendship, the two had disagreements. At one point, as they prepared to get back out on the road again and visit the churches they'd established, they clashed over who might go along with them. Barnabas wanted to bring his cousin John Mark, but there was a touchy backstory. John Mark had "deserted them in Pamphylia and had not continued with them in the work." (Acts 15:38) It's understandable that Paul resented what had happened, but that's not how Barnabas saw it.

> They had such a sharp disagreement that they parted company. Barnabas took Mark and sailed for Cyprus, but Paul chose Silas and left, commended by the believers to the grace of the LORD.
> Acts 15:39–40

What to make of this phase of their friendship? We know from hints in the letters of Paul that their disagreements didn't last forever. Paul wrote his letter to the Corinthians long after he and Barnabas had parted ways, and he mentioned Barnabas as a fellow evangelist who worked with his hands. Paul was defending their right to receive some financial support from the communities they supported spiritually:

> This is my defense to those who sit in judgment on me. Don't we have the right to food and drink? Don't we have the right to take a believing wife along with us, as do the other apostles and the Lord's brothers and Cephas? Or is it only I and Barnabas who lack the right to not work for a living?
> 1 Corinthians 9:3–6

Even though they were no longer traveling together, Paul clearly still thought highly of his friend.

Just as Paul and Barnabas gave us the model of working for the Gospel side by side, they also showed us that friends can disagree and still respect each other. The dispute they had was not inconsequential; it was a substantive disagreement over how the Gospel might best be served, and by whom. The evidence in Paul's letters tells us that they were able to disagree and move on without nurturing resentment toward each other. In fact, in later years John Mark was mentioned by Paul with approval (Colossians 4:10), suggesting that the friction between them had been put to rest. Paul urged that John Mark be welcomed.

The friendships that laid the foundation for Paul's missionary journeys and the birth of the Christian church were real relationships, among real people. They had ups and downs, joys and misunderstandings. Paul and Barnabas were able to hold on to their respect for one another because they kept their focus on Jesus, not on their own pride and self-will. Whatever the frustrations between Barnabas and Paul, we know their work was successful—in part—because of their partnership in those early years of the church.

Aquila and Priscilla (Acts 18:1–21, 18:24–26)

Paul had many other partners in his missionary activity, and those relationships continued to sustain him. As you'll also see, those friendships multiplied and spread into networks of people out sharing the love and truth of Jesus. One of the longest layovers in Paul's missionary journeys was in Corinth, where he stayed for a year and a half. Paul had left Athens and traveled to Corinth, where he encountered a man and wife who became crucial to his work there. Aquila and his wife Priscilla (Acts 18:2-3) were Christian refugees from Rome, where they had been expelled along with most other Jews by order of Emperor Claudius. Paul had much in common with them. Like him, they were Jews who came from Asia Minor, not from Judea, and like him they were tentmakers.

It was almost certainly the case that Aquila and Priscilla had been in Corinth for some time before Paul arrived, and that they already had an established tentmaking business—a prosperous industry in the ancient world, where travelers always needed portable shelter. Practicing a trade in the ancient world, especially an established trade like tentmaking, meant joining the local guild and becoming part of the local trade network. It's unlikely an itinerant like Paul would have been able to do that, so he was probably taken on as a worker in Aquila and Priscilla's shop. They also invited him into their home, so we know that they were generous, hospitable, and willing to do whatever they could to help Paul with his mission.

During this time in Corinth, two other key figures in the early church—Silas and Timothy—came to visit as well. Once that happened, we're told Paul was freed up to devote himself to "testifying to the Jews that Jesus was the Christ" (Acts 18:5), but not all of them wanted to hear the message. Some became "abusive," but the Lord spoke to Paul in a dream telling him not to be afraid.

"... keep on speaking, do not be silent. For I am with you, and no one is going to attack and harm you, because I have many people in this city." So Paul stayed in Corinth for a year and a half, teaching them the word of God.

Acts 18:9b-11

Buoyed by the friendship and support of Priscilla and Aquila, Paul continued to preach—even as he came under repeated attacks.

These friends were so committed to Paul's mission that he took them with him as his partners on the next leg of his journey, staying on in Ephesus with the believers there (Acts 18:18). We know that Priscilla and Aquila became leaders in the Ephesian church, instructing those who had yet to encounter the fullness of the faith:

> Meanwhile a Jew named Apollos, a native of Alexandria, came to Ephesus. He was a learned man, with a thorough knowledge of the Scriptures. He had been instructed in the way of the LORD, and he spoke with great fervor and taught about Jesus accurately, though he knew only the baptism of John. He began to speak boldly in the synagogue. When Priscilla and Aquila heard him, they invited him to their home and explained to him the way of God more adequately.
>
> Acts 19: 24-26

Just as they had done with Paul, Priscilla and Aquila took him into their own home.

And though this part isn't talked about much in the Bible, we see in the friendship between the three of them the grace of sharing a friend with your spouse. Aquila and Priscilla are always mentioned together, never separately. Having a female friend might have been a novel experience for the unmarried Paul, and his unmarried status made him an unlikely friend in the ancient world for a married couple. Aquila and Priscilla must have been very dear to Paul, and his bond with them unlike any of his other friendships.

For the married folks reading these words, how much of an effort do you make to include single friends in your community of fellowship? Sheldon and I have one single friend in particular who feels like such a gift to us! I never think of him in terms of his marital status. I just love that we both have topics we love to debate and discuss with him. He loves Sheldon's cooking, and we love to eat out together too. He is one of our dearest friends, and we both cherish him as individuals and as a couple. We all laugh together and have some very thought-provoking conversations too. Our lives are immeasurably better because this friend has been in them for fifteen years. I hope he feels the same way about us! Single friends, do you seek out healthy couples to include in your circle? Your perspectives on life, church, culture, and trials are crucial to informing others. Your viewpoint and companionship have enormous value and add critical insights to important conversations.

Wherever Paul traveled, people were drawn to him and encouraged in the faith. The New Testament is full of their names: Epaphras and Tychicus and Apphia and Zenas the lawyer and Aristarchus and Archippus and so many others—the growing family of early believers sustained by friendship and mutual devotion. We know of others who were even closer to him, and to whom he wrote letters: Timothy, whose Jewish mother and Greek father meant he was half-in, half-out of the Jewish world, and who was a spiritual son to Paul. There was also Titus, who was his second-in-command and deputy at Corinth when that church hit troubled times. Silas shared prison with him. And there was Luke, the beloved physician who accompanied him on the journeys with Silas, as well as on his final journey to Rome. What a beautiful network of support Paul had in the midst of a demanding ministry.

Onesimus (Book of Philemon)

But it is Paul's friendship with Onesimus that gives us deeper insights into Paul's heart. The shortest book in the New Testament is Paul's letter to Philemon, Onesimus's master. In the twenty-five verses of Philemon, we see Paul's gentleness, compassion, and justice. Written probably from his imprisonment in Rome—Paul called himself "an old man and now also a prisoner of Christ Jesus." (Philemon v. 9) Paul was pleading for the freedom of the slave Onesimus. We have no way of knowing the exact circumstances of how Paul encountered the man. Reading between the lines, it sounds like Onesimus may have run away from his master, whom Paul knew. It's also possible he had been sent to Paul by Philemon. Slaves were often sent on errands by their "owners," and from the context of the letter it seems that Philemon knew Paul was in prison. Philemon may have sent Onesimus to Paul to be of service in any way he could.

But Paul had begun to imagine a different world. While under house arrest in Rome, far from his home and his community, Paul had gotten to know Onesimus. Paul didn't view him as a useful appliance, an object to be loaned or disposed of, but as a human being. Paul preached the Gospel to Onesimus, and Onesimus believed. Just like Mary who sat at the feet of Jesus, setting aside menial tasks out of love for her Lord, Onesimus sat at the feet of Paul. And just as Jesus had done with Mary, Paul did not turn him away and remind him of his "place." He shared Christ with him as he would have with anyone else, and when Onesimus accepted Christ, he became Paul's spiritual son. In literal Greek, Paul wrote, "I gave birth to him."

To us that might seem like a usual thing—of course he was Paul's spiritual son! But in the ancient world a slave would not have been referred to in that way. A slave could not be anyone's son, because he was not legally a person. He could not own property, he could not give testimony in any court, and if he earned any money doing the tasks that were set him, that money belonged by legal right to his "owner."

Paul recognized that in Christ, a new relationship had begun. He called Onesimus something he called no one else in the New Testament: "my very heart." (Philemon v. 12) Paul wanted to give Philemon the chance to do the right thing, and to recognize this new relationship in Christ for what it truly was:

> Perhaps the reason he was separated from you for a little while was that you might have him back forever—no longer as a slave, but better than a slave, as a dear brother. He is very dear to me but even dearer to you, both as a fellow man and as a brother in the LORD.
> Philemon 15–16

Paul called Onesimus what he was: a "fellow man" and "a brother in the Lord." Paul wrote a careful, loving, diplomatic letter as if he were writing to two quarreling brothers, not to a master and a slave.

Onesimus is also mentioned at the end of Paul's letter to the Colossians, where he was designated as the bearer of the letter along with Tychicus. Together they were instructed to tell the believers at Colossae everything that had happened with Paul in Rome, and Onesimus was referred to as "our faithful and dear brother." (Colossians 4:9) He was a key figure in the Christian community, one of the few entrusted to take personal greetings and messages from Paul himself.

That word "faithful" was at the heart of all Paul's friendships: Christ's love and truth were at the core. The Lord was the common thread in his community, and love of Jesus was what sustained their bonds. Paul shows us that when we share Jesus with someone we love, that connection becomes unbreakable—even in the face of disagreements or catastrophe. The other half of that "faithful" is what happens when we keep Jesus at the center. We are committed to each other, in the same way that Jesus is faithful to us. We don't give up on people. We expect good things from them. We believe in their ability to do great things. We trust them with our heart, and we share with them what God is calling us to do, trusting that they will help us get there. We face hardships together. Most of all, Paul teaches us that the truest friendship—like the deepest love—is one that finds its beginning, end, and purpose in Jesus, no matter how far from home we wander or what journeys God calls us to undertake.

Prayer: Heavenly Father, thank you for the friends You send into our lives to help us navigate our journeys. Whether we stay close to home or travel the globe, may we take Your faithfulness and truth to everyone we meet. We are grateful for those who will walk the extra mile with us, pray for us, and encourage us when we need it most. Please remind us to be that kind of friend to others, seeking the good and forgiving the bad. Help us to include all kinds of people in our lives and to pour into theirs Your love, grace, and mercy.

JOB AND HIS FRIENDS

Companions in Grief

The Book of Job

I'll never forget that phone call. I was preparing to cover for my colleague, Bret Baier, and anchor his 6 P.M. show *Special Report*. I saw my brother's name pop up on my cellphone, but the show was about to start. *I'll just call him after.* But it rang again. And again. I realized whatever it was needed my attention. The floor dropped out from underneath me when I did pick up and he said, "Dad's dead." All I can remember is yelling, "No!" over and over. My co-workers ran to see what was happening and quickly figured it out as I begged my brother for details. He'd apparently died peacefully in his sleep, but it was totally unexpected, and I was reeling. The first few days passed in a haze of tears and confusion, but the heartbreak was just beginning.

My father had drafted a will, but never signed it. There were more loose ends than I could ever have imagined, and if not for two of his closest friends I would have drowned in the legal wrangling. One helped me get the paperwork filed with the court system so that I could be appointed executor and begin untangling the mess. These men became my angels on earth. Just as they had walked through every joy and every struggle with my father when he was alive, they selflessly worked around the clock to help his shell-shocked daughter. I felt I really didn't have the luxury of grieving in those first couple of years, overwhelmed with court hearings and financial documents. They sustained me until I could catch my breath.

One of those men had been through some very dark days himself, and my father stood by him. Their bond went beyond mere friendship, as their relationship had been cemented in the deepest of valleys. He was incredibly kind to repay the debt to me. I was also carried along by my friend Emily, who constantly checked on me and gave me the best advice: *Just do the next thing.* I couldn't imagine how I would ever get out from under the crushing weight of trying to settle the chaotic estate, much less the unanswered questions and grief that plagued me day and night. Emily was right, and she was steady when I was losing it. Of course, none of this would have held together without the rock-solid support of my husband, Sheldon.

Friends show up in so many ways in our daily lives, but sometimes it takes a real crisis to see the full blessing of their presence and kind words. They aren't perfect; none of us is. But a true friend's intentions are always pure, even if they fumble in their efforts to comfort us. That's at the heart of the Old Testament story of Job's grief and the friends who showed up in his darkest hour. Over the years, Job—the person and the book—has come to be associated with suffering, the meaning behind it, and the inscrutable ways of God. When most people talk about Job's friends, it's primarily to criticize them. The reason is simple: When bad things happened to Job, his friends wound up lecturing him on how his suffering was likely his fault.

At first glance, the structure of the book of Job seems simple: In response to his suffering, Job cursed the very fact of his birth, his friends blamed Job, and at the end of the book God appeared and said, "You're all wrong." But the book is actually a lot more complicated than that, and so is Job's relationship with his friends. For one thing—Eliphaz, Bildad, and Zophar—all had slightly different points of view. For another, they weren't simply sitting around lecturing Job; they were trying to help him wrestle with the meaning of what had happened in his life. Not everything they said was true or accurate, but the fact that they showed up and struggled to engage with these problems alongside him makes this book an extended meditation not just on suffering but on friendship.

But back to the beginning. Job likely lived during the time of the patriarchs, before the nation of Israel was formed from Abraham, Isaac, and Jacob. Historians believe the book dates to a time after the Tower of Babel disaster, when men found out they were no match for God Almighty. Keeping that timeframe in mind sheds light on the book of Job and the discussions in it. It means that everyone in this portion of Scripture—Job, Eliphaz, Bildad, and Zophar—was reasoning about a God they knew from observing the beauty of creation and from hearing stories passed down through generations, but not from seeing firsthand His supernatural action on behalf of His people. They didn't yet have the example of God's miracles performed on behalf of Israel to rely on—no parting of the Red Sea, no law given at Sinai, no manna in the wilderness. But while they didn't have the advantage of knowing God in the context of His covenant with Israel, they did know God.

We know that Job was a "blameless and upright" man who "feared God and shunned evil," (Job 1:1) and that reminds us that a connection with God is always possible. Job's relationship with God was so strong that God called him "my servant" (Job 1:8) and commended him in front of Satan and the heavenly court. That's what actually set the whole plot of the book in motion, because the minute God praised Job in front of Satan, the evil one was determined to prove God wrong.

> "Does Job fear God for nothing?" Satan replied. "Have you not put a hedge around him and his household and everything he has? You have blessed the work of his hands, so that his flocks and herds are spread throughout the land. But now stretch out your hand and strike everything he has, and he will surely curse you to your face." The LORD said to Satan, "Very well, then, everything he has is in your power, but on the man himself do not lay a finger."
> Job 1:9-12

Satan's question was an uncomfortable one, and it can—and should—make us squirm today. It's a question we need to ask ourselves: *Do I fear God just because of what I'd lose if I didn't? When I look around at my life and see the many blessings God has given me—home and family and fulfilling work—does that increase my love and respect for God? Or do I only love and trust Him when things are good? What would my relationship with God be like if those things were all taken away?*

Those are the kinds of deeply troublesome questions most of us tamp down rather than work through. They require gut-level honesty, an unflinching look in the mirror. But there are moments in life when nearly all of us will confront these questions head on, times when we are completely unmoored and broken-hearted. It could be that devastating phone call or knock at the door. It could be a loved one so far down the path of addiction that you see no way to pull them back out. Maybe it's a betrayal so deep and shocking that you're questioning everything about your life as you thought you knew it.

I remember years ago watching a Bible study video by Beth Moore. She took us there. She urged each of us to think about the thing we fear most in life, the absolute worst-case scenario. I have spent lots of time there in my head. There's something that tells me if I think through the most awful things, my system is somehow prepared—you know—just in case they actually show up. But that definitely wasn't Beth's point. At the end of that darkest place you can imagine one thing will absolutely be true: God will not have changed and He'll still be there. Once we know the security of eternity, we can accept that our path between here and there may be excruciatingly difficult at times. Not long after Satan vowed to break him, Job's life completely fell apart.

Job's losses were unimaginable. Raiding parties carried off all the wealth of his flocks, and a storm collapsed the house of his eldest son—where all of his children were feasting together—killing them all at once. Job accepted his losses with a kind of humility and grace I bet few of us could match.

> At this, Job got up and tore his robe and shaved his head. Then he fell to the ground in worship and said:
> "Naked I came from my mother's womb,
> and naked I will depart.
> The LORD gave and the LORD has taken away;
> may the name of the LORD be praised."

In all this, Job did not sin by charging God with wrong-doing.
Job 1:20–22

But Satan wasn't done with his evil experiment just yet. So he went back to God to ask for permission to attack where humans are often most vulnerable: our health.

"Skin for skin!" Satan replied. "A man will give all he has for his own life. But now stretch out your hand and strike his flesh and bones, and he will surely curse you to your face." The LORD said to Satan, "Very well, then, he is in your hands; but you must spare his life." So Satan went out from the presence of the LORD and afflicted Job with painful sores from the soles of his feet to the crown of his head.
Job 2:4–7

Job's wife—who is not named in the story—urged him to just give up, to "curse God and die." No doubt she was devastated over their unthinkable losses too. But Job told her, "You are talking like a foolish woman. Shall we accept good from God, and not trouble?" (Job 2:10) We can all understand why she was in such pain, and sometimes our spouse will not be the best source of wisdom and comfort to us. In this scenario, that's likely why Job's friends became even more important to him.

It's at the point that Job had lost everything and was in deep physical and emotional pain that his friends showed up.

When Job's three friends, Eliphaz the Temanite, Bildad the Shuhite, and Zophar the Naamathite heard about all the troubles that had come upon him, they set out from their homes and met together by agreement to go and sympathize with him and comfort him. When they saw him from a distance, they could hardly recognize him; they began to weep aloud, and they tore their robes and sprinkled dust on their heads. Then they sat on the ground with him for seven days and seven nights. No one said a word to him, because they saw how great his suffering was.

Job 2:11–13

Let's unpack the beautiful things these three friends did, because each of their actions was significant. They heard about everything that had happened to Job, and instead of rushing over to be with him they "met together by agreement" before they went to see him. Why? Well, meeting beforehand may have allowed them to think about how they wanted to approach Job and what they could possibly say to him. It allowed them to put Job and his needs first by being intentional about their visit. It showed a unity among the three of them. Their plan was to "sympathize with him and comfort him." What better goal could any confidant have?

But look at what happened when they arrived to help. As prepared as they might have thought they were, when they laid eyes on their disfigured friend the reality of it hit them so hard that they wept aloud, tore their robes, and sprinkled dust on their heads. These were all the ritual actions of grief in the ancient world. They joined in his agony with him. No one told him to get it together. They fell apart with him. Job's sorrow wasn't something they observed from the outside but an event that they willingly entered along with him.

Next, they did the most important thing they could have: nothing. For seven days and seven nights "no one said a word to him, because they saw how great his suffering was." (Job 2:13) No platitudes were offered, no easy explanations, no assurances it would all make sense one day. Silence can indicate not only respect, but also humility—acknowledging the unknowable purposes of God, before the immensity of someone else's grief, before the sacredness of that space and time.

Job's friends showed up and offered the gifts of presence, shared grief, and silence. So often when someone we know has suffered a terrible loss we hesitate to reach out because we feel awkward or worry our words will come out all wrong. Just do it. Looking away from a friend's pain will always be the wrong strategy. Plunge into the anguish with them. Just show up. In their fog of despair, they're unlikely to remember your words anyway. But they will always remember that you were present. "Mourn with those who mourn," in the words of Paul (Romans 12:15).

The First Discussion

Job finally spoke, and when he broke his silence, it was not to lash out at God but to curse his own birth. Job wished he had never been born. "Why did I not perish at birth, and die as I came forth from the womb?" (Job 3:11) he asked, in despair. Failing that, he wondered why he was not allowed to die when he was young, resting where no sorrow could touch him anymore. "I have no peace, no happiness," he proclaims. "I have no rest, but only turmoil." (Job 3:11, 26)

Job's friend Eliphaz was the first to speak to him, and he addressed Job's despair before anything else. He reminded Job that he had been a leader and a teacher of many, but added "trouble comes to you, and you are discouraged; it strikes you, and you are dismayed." (Job 4:5) Unfortunately, Eliphaz seemed to suggest that Job wasn't following the same advice he'd given to others. When reading the book of Job we must remember that—in the end—God ultimately told these friends they were wrong, and He called their attempts to comfort Job "folly." (Job 42:8)

> Eliphaz was just getting started:
> Consider now: Who, being innocent, has ever perished?
> Where were the upright ever destroyed?
> As I have observed, those who plow evil
> and those who sow trouble reap it.
> At the breath of God they perish;
> at the blast of his anger they are no more.
> Job 4:7–9

This is some beautiful poetry, like most of the book of Job, but there is something very un-beautiful lurking within it. "Where were the upright ever destroyed?" Eliphaz asked, implying that because Job had suffered such great loss, he must not be upright. Eliphaz assumed Job's staggering losses were punishment for something Job did wrong. Eliphaz then recommended a course of action for Job: "If I were you," he said, "I would appeal to God; I would lay my cause before him." (Job 5:8) What he as a mortal human could not know was that Job was actually targeted by the enemy and living through this anguish precisely *because* God had pointed out just how upright Job was.

Finally, Eliphaz counseled Job that he should look upon the ruination of his life as the loving correction of God:

Blessed is the one whom God corrects;
so do not despise the discipline of the Almighty.
For he wounds, but he also binds up;
he injures, but his hands also heal.
    Job 5:17–18

There is never a suggestion in Scripture that any of Job's friends approached him with anything but the purest of intentions, but can you imagine worse advice for a grieving friend? It's hard to fathom saying these things to someone in our own lives who had just lost a child or who was suffering from a terminal illness.

This idea that Job's misfortune was the direct result of his sinfulness was the theme that ran through all of the so-called advice Job's friends attempted to give him throughout the book. Job's friend Bildad added to the wounds by suggesting that it wasn't just Job who had violated God's commands, but also Job's children. "When your children sinned against him," Bildad said, "he gave them over to the penalty of their sin." (Job 8:4) If these remarks seem cruel to us—good. We have the benefit of knowing exactly why Job was suffering, but his friends didn't. We should never authoritatively assume we know why any human being is allowed to walk into a season of despair.

Jesus addressed the connection between sinfulness and suffering in the Gospel of Luke, when He was asked about some Galilean Jews who had recently been put to death in Jerusalem by Pilate:

Now there were some present at that time who told Jesus about the Galileans whose blood Pilate had mixed with their sacrifices. Jesus answered, "Do you think that these Galileans were worse sinners than all the other Galileans because they suffered this way? I tell you, no! But unless you repent, you too will all perish. Or those eighteen who died when the tower in Siloam fell on them—do you think they were more guilty than all the others living in Jerusalem? I tell you, no! But unless you repent, you too will all perish."

Luke 13:1-5

Jesus emphatically rejected the idea that these deaths happened to these particular people because they were somehow worse sinners than everybody else in Jerusalem. He mentioned two instances of death: one caused by the cruelty of other human beings and one caused by natural disaster, to show that neither of them happened because of the sin of the victims.

When Jesus warned His listeners that they might perish unless they repented, He was cautioning them that they could lose the possibility of eternal life in heaven unless they prepared their souls. It was not the assessment of this world, for good or ill, that He was telling them to be concerned about. The only judgment that mattered was the one that would come after this life. As he often did, Jesus took a question that had been posed to Him and invited His listeners to see it from a different perspective and in a new way. What if the judgment of God on sinners happened not in this world but in the next?

But Job's friends lacked this perspective, because their view of life was confined to this world alone. In this context, we realize that everything they said to Job made sense to them! They knew that God was just; therefore, they assumed all the suffering Job was experiencing had to be a fair judgment. There had to be a reason for their friend's despair. They thought it was their responsibility to help Job find that reason and fix it. But Jesus taught us that suffering is not always connected to a person's sin, and that the fate we need to be worried about is that of our own soul. Jesus pulled the focus of His listeners away from thinking about other people, and redirected them to think instead about their own lives.

Job's friends had this problem. They thought they were offering support by helping Job figure out where he had gone wrong; they only ended up causing him more pain. But the worst was yet to come. When Job resisted their simplistic explanations for his suffering and persisted in his despair, his friends grew frustrated—and they expressed it openly. Have you been on the receiving end of this misplaced anger? Maybe you've been the one who unleashed it. Oh, that we would stop and think that through.

This brings someone specific to mind for me. He is struggling—mightily. He makes bad decisions and has for years. I used to think he was just immature, but I've seen him deteriorate into mental illness. I've lost count of the bridges he's burned and the people he's alienated. Most people who know him have given up, some have become openly hostile toward him. He has said and done things to offend numerous people who have tried to help him. My frustration isn't with what he says and does, but with the illness that is now obviously controlling his mind. I'm not a professional, and I've tried to connect him with people who can help him. I'm not the only one. But most people have bowed out, tired of what they view as his manipulations. I've drawn clear boundaries with him, but I still respond when he reaches out because I know he desperately needs help. I can understand why many others view him the way Job's friends did—as if he is unable to admit his own faults and is now being punished by God.

Job's friend Zophar was probably the worst offender in the anger department:

> Then Zophar the Naamathite replied:
>   "Are all these words to go unanswered?
>   Is this talker to be vindicated?
>   Will your idle talk reduce others to silence?
>   Will no one rebuke you when you mock?
>   You say to God, 'My beliefs are flawless
>   and I am pure in your sight.'
>   Oh, how I wish that God would speak,
>   that he would open his lips against you
>   and disclose to you the secrets of wisdom."
>   Job 11:1-6

Zophar arrived to comfort his friend, but ten chapters later, he was longing for Job to be rebuked. It can be frustrating when our friends don't give us the emotional response we think they should, but there is often something else going on. By steadily resisting their explanations for his suffering, Job was challenging more than just his friends' ability to be good comforters. He was questioning everything they thought they knew about God and the universe. He was suggesting that their ideas might be wrong. That's an uncomfortable place to be, so his friends reacted in anger, frustration, and even confusion.

In response, Job suggested that their view of God might just be too small:

> To God belong wisdom and power;
>   counsel and understanding are his.
> What he tears down cannot be rebuilt;
>   those he imprisons cannot be released.
> If he holds back the waters, there is drought;
>   if he lets them loose, they devastate the land.
> To him belong strength and insight;
>   both deceived and deceiver are his.
> He leads rulers away stripped
>   and makes fools of judges.
> He takes off the shackles put on by kings
>   and ties a loincloth around their waist.
> He leads priests away stripped
>   and overthrows officials long established.
> He silences the lips of trusted advisers
>   and takes away the discernment of elders.
> He pours contempt on nobles
>   and disarms the mighty.
> Job 12:13-21

If we know anything about God, it is that He often defies worldly understanding and expectations. God impoverishes the rulers of this world and brings down the mighty from their seats of power. Any source of earthly wisdom and power is feeble foolishness to Him—and so, Job implied, all our ideas about God are exactly that: mere thoughts. We are not prepared to understand the inscrutable mystery of God's personhood, because we are too weak to hold His awesomeness in our minds, no matter how wise we think we are. Deuteronomy 29:29 tells us, "The secret things belong to the Lord our God."

In his final word to his friends, Job brought a shattering charge: He said that God had denied him justice (Job 27:2). What a shocking thing to say! Sometimes when people are in immense pain and grief, they become angry with God. They might hurl their rage at God and say things we might be tempted to respond to or even to refute. The book of Job shows us the folly of that, not just emotionally but theologically. Because here's the thing: Job was right. God *had* denied him justice. Nothing that had happened to Job was just or deserved. If this world was all that existed (as Job probably believed), then he was right: There was no justice for him in this world. But God always has the final word.

End of the Debate

Just as we learn from the examples of love stories gone wrong, we can also glean valuable insights from relationships that weren't exactly models of ideal friendships. Often the best lessons come from seeing where someone else messed things up—even people who act with the best intentions, as Job's friends did. When we show up for a friend in pain, it is never our job to authoritatively pronounce exactly what God is doing. When someone in deep grief asks *why,* we shouldn't feel compelled to say something beyond what is often the honest truth: "I don't know."

As Christians, we have a Savior who knows our suffering intimately because He Himself experienced it. God does not stand outside our pain and promise to make it disappear. God stands with us *in* our suffering. Jesus experienced rejection, grief, and physical agony. The knowledge of those experiences did not leave Him when He ascended to heaven. He has lived our pain.

In the darkest period of my life, living through years of a missed diagnosis and excruciating, chronic pain I cried out to God countless times. Though He blessed me with a doctor who finally figured out what I was dealing with, I was plunged into a dark hole of despair when that physician said the words, "There is no cure." That was where I hit rock bottom. It was the one time I felt God speak directly to me, and the words I heard weren't, "I'm going to heal you!" What I heard unmistakably was, "I will be with you." And He has been. It's through the soul-crushing emotional and physical pain that I've suffered that I can now assure others who grieve. *You are not alone. I will sit here with you, and God will never abandon His child.*

We won't always have the right words. We will get things wrong. Eliphaz, Bildad, and Zophar spoke in error, and God was not happy about it:

> After the Lord had said these things to Job, he said to Eliphaz the Temanite, "I am angry with you and your two friends, because you have not spoken the truth about me, as my servant Job has. So now take seven bulls and seven rams and go to my servant Job and sacrifice a burnt offering for yourselves. My servant Job will pray for you, and I will accept his prayer and not deal with you according to your folly. You have not spoken the truth about me, as my servant Job has." So Eliphaz the Temanite, Bildad the

Shuhite and Zophar the Naamathite did what the LORD
told them; and the LORD accepted Job's prayer.
　Job 42:7–9

Job's friends were way off base, but they cared enough to show
up when he'd lost everything. They'd attempted, in their own human wisdom, to reach conclusions about his suffering and how
to resolve it. In the end, God Himself showed up to defend Job.

That highlights the importance of putting God at the center
of our friendships. Job and his friends all agreed that the focus
should be on the Lord's purpose in the midst of the devastation.
They might have disagreed about where God was, and they might
have drawn faulty conclusions about the answer, but at least their
conversation was headed in the right direction. What about in
our lives? How do we respond when our friends challenge us on
spiritual matters? Do we insist that our own views of God and
why He acts must be the right ones, or do we have a heart open
enough to listen for the ways God may speak to us through our
friends? Job also put faith at the core of these relationships by
interceding for his friends. Time and again the Bible shows us the
power of intercessory prayer.

Eventually, Job was fully restored—and then some! We're told
God "gave him twice as much as he had before." (Job 42:10) Just
as losing everything wasn't a punishment on Job, his new family
and wealth wasn't a reward of some kind. Job had knock-down,
drag out, painfully honest conversations with both God and his
earthly friends. Genuine relationships can handle those storms.
It's the courage to actually show up and engage that defines a
solid friendship.

Prayer: Lord God, grant me the strength to be a true friend to those in grief. Guard my heart and my tongue. Help me to sit in silence. Help me to look for Your paths and Your purposes in the midst of sorrow, and to be honest when those are hard to find. Teach me to be a voice of comfort to those who mourn.

Friends for Eternity

Luke 5:1–11, Mark 3:13–19, Mark 9:38–40,
Luke 9:51–55, 1 John 4:7–16, Mark 8:27–30,
Matthew 26:36–46, Matthew 20:20–28, John
19:25–27, John 20:3–10, Revelation 1:10–18

In coming to take on a human body and live among us, experiencing all that earthly life entails, Christ showed us how to live while fully embracing both the spiritual and the physical elements of life. Jesus spoke many powerful truths in order to guide us into holiness, but His relationships speak just as eloquently about His nature. He was God, and He had close friends.

Jesus' friendships teach us just as His parables and sermons do.

As a youngster, when I was beginning to learn slightly more challenging piano pieces, I remember one songbook in particular that had a jazzed-up arrangement of "What a Friend We Have in Jesus." A church hymnal still sits on my piano today. The lyrics fill my heart and my mind with such encouragement and assurance. That song in particular locked itself into my memory decades ago, and what comfort it brings now. "In His arms He'll take and shield you; you will find a solace there," is among the many promises woven into the melody. It isn't just a lofty song that doesn't connect to our real lives. Just as He is to us today, Christ was a friend and companion to those who shared his earthly journey centuries ago.

Friendships are part of the human experience. God created us for community, and Jesus was no exception when He walked among us in human flesh. Christ's ministry was spread through strong relationships, forged in both grace and persecution. Jesus built His life around those friendships and left us a model of human love we can apply today. In Him we see how seeds of connection, watered with selflessness and intention, can blossom into unbreakable bonds.

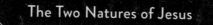

The Two Natures of Jesus

One of Jesus' closest friends—perhaps even the closest, according to the testimony of the Gospels, was the apostle John. John was near to Jesus in His life, in His death, and in His resurrection, in a way that none of Jesus' other disciples were. John's relationship with Christ illustrates two things: how to be close to Him in a spiritual sense and how to walk with Him as a friend. Much of our information about John and his relationship with Jesus comes from the book of John. Five times in that Gospel, John used the phrase "the disciple whom Jesus loved" to describe himself (John 13:23, 19:26, 20:2, 21:7, and 21:20). Instead of pointing him out as someone uniquely special, this description seems to be John's attempt to minimize his own role in the narrative, modestly reducing himself to someone defined by his relationship with Jesus, instead of by his own name.

It appears John was marked by humility. It wasn't about him. But it's also important to think about the words he chose to describe himself. The verb for "loved" is one of two verbs: it is either *agape* or *phileo*. The definition of *agape* is the deep spiritual love that sees the object of that love just as God sees them, the sort of love that seeks only the good of the beloved one—a divine love, rooted in a shared love of God. *Phileo* love is the deep affection of friendship, the kind of love that finds joy in companionship with the beloved. It's the kind of human love we normally associate with our closest friends. If Matthew emphasized Jesus' kingship, Mark focused on His servanthood, and Luke on His humanity. John was the writer who, from the first words of his Gospel, underlined Jesus' divinity.

Jesus was both a friend to His disciples and the Lord to be praised. And He gave a very clear roadmap for both connecting with Him and being a true friend.

My command is this: Love each other as I have loved you. Greater love has no one than this: to lay down one's life for one's friends. You are my friends if you do what I command. I no longer call you servants, because a servant does not know his master's business. Instead, I have called you friends, for everything that I learned from my Father I have made known to you.
John 15:12-15

First, we are to love others just the way Christ did. He was totally selfless, something we should strive for in our own relationships. Jesus also told us nothing could be greater than sacrificing our own lives for others. Little did they know just how literal that statement would be. Christ also called us to follow His commands, a show of humble obedience. Finally, He broke down any distance between Himself and His followers. *You're not just someone at arm's length; you are truly my friends.*

We see how Jesus and the disciples, and other close friends, did life in community. Think about how well you get to know someone when you travel together. That's what they were almost always doing once His ministry kicked off. They shared their meals, found places to stay and walked through experiences like exhaustion and hunger. Those are the kinds of things that strip away any pretense. That's when you see a person's true character.

Their situation makes me think of one of my favorite TV shows, *The Amazing Race*. It puts pairs of people together—co-workers, family members, friends, romantic partners—and sends them chasing an epic collection of clues all over the globe. Everyone starts out in cute matching outfits or with a heartwarming story about how they met. But it's when you're out of cash and forced to eat scorpion eyeballs in some distant land where you can't speak the language that things get ugly—quick! We have watched some legendary meltdowns. As thrilling as I think it would be to undertake the *Amazing Race* challenge, there's not a single meaningful relationship in my life I'd be willing to put under that kind of stress! But stressful conditions were where Jesus and His disciples lived and worked together. And through that lens we witness Christ's care for those closest to Him.

Son of Thunder, Apostle of Love

Who was this John whom Jesus loved? Most scholars believe John was the younger brother of James, who would be the first apostle to die a martyr's death. John was a fisherman on the Sea of Galilee. He and James were business partners with another pair of brothers, Simon Peter and Andrew. Jesus called all four men when they were in their boats along the shore. Andrew and Peter had met Jesus before (John 1:35–42), but it was not until this encounter at the Sea of Galilee that He invited them to full-time ministry.

> He got into one of the boats, the one belonging to Simon, and asked him to put out a little from shore. Then he sat down and taught the people from the boat. When he had finished speaking, he said to Simon, "Put out into deep water, and let down the nets for a catch." Simon answered, "Master, we've worked hard all night and haven't caught anything. But because you say so, I will let down the nets." When they had done so, they caught such a large number of fish that their nets began to break. So they signaled their partners in the other boat to come and help them, and they came and filled both boats so full that they began to sink. When Simon Peter saw this, he fell at Jesus' knees and said, "Go away from me, LORD; I am a sinful man!" For he and all his companions were astonished at the catch of fish they had taken, and so were James and John, the sons of Zebedee, Simon's partners.
>
> Luke 5:3–10

By granting the men a miraculous catch of fish, Jesus showed that His supernatural power could change the everyday course of their lives. It may be easier to ignore God's call on our lives when it's all in grandiose spiritual language, but it's a lot harder when there are hundreds of flopping fish pouring into the boat! Jesus went on to use a fishing metaphor when He responded to Peter's fear: "Don't be afraid; from now on you will fish for people." (Luke 5:10b)

Jesus loved to do this, express deep truths in everyday illustrations that His human companions could grasp. In the same way that He took on flesh in order to reveal God to us, He cloaked complicated ideas in relatable parables. And finally Peter, who'd already known Jesus for a while at this point, really "got it" for the first time! So did his friends, James and John. All four men—Peter, Andrew, James, and John—"Pulled their boats up on shore, left everything and followed him." (Luke 5:11)

But as we'll see, James and John's attraction to Jesus leaned heavily on what "astonished" them in this encounter: supernatural power. To that point, John was not always the wisest of Jesus' disciples. In fact, he could be a bit of a hothead! We know that John was full of passion, because Jesus Himself told us so. In the Gospel of Mark, take a look at what happened when Jesus marked out twelve of His disciples to be apostles.

Jesus went up on a mountainside and called to him those he wanted, and they came to him. He appointed twelve that they might be with him and that he might send them out to preach and to have authority to drive out demons. These are the twelve he appointed: Simon (to whom he gave the name Peter), James son of Zebedee and his brother John (to them he gave the name Boanerges, which means "sons of thunder"), Andrew, Philip, Bartholomew, Matthew, Thomas, James son of Alphaeus, Thaddaeus, Simon the Zealot, and Judas Iscariot, who betrayed him.

Mark 3:13–19

Jesus Himself gave James and John the nickname "sons of thunder." From the very beginning of His ministry, Jesus knew who these men really were. They were fiery and full of zeal and sometimes a little too ready to call down the wrath of God on people who disagreed with them. But none of that disqualified them from being Jesus' friends and followers.

When the apostles returned from the first mission Jesus had sent them on, they were full of fervor and of amazement at the power of God—perhaps no one more so than John the firebrand.

"Teacher," said John, "we saw someone driving out demons in your name and we told him to stop, because he was not one of us."

"Do not stop him," Jesus said. "For no one who does a miracle in my name can in the next moment say anything bad about me, for whoever is not against us is for us."

Mark 9:38–40

In his eagerness to defend Jesus' honor and reputation, John had intervened and told someone to stop using Jesus' name to heal people. Jesus had to gently remind John that His inner circle didn't have a monopoly on invoking the name of Christ to accomplish holy things. He urged John not to see the disciples' closeness to Jesus as excluding others. He went on, "Truly I tell you, anyone who gives you a cup of water in my name because you belong to the Messiah will certainly not lose their reward." (Mark 9:41)

Apparently, the lesson wasn't fully absorbed because the very next thing that happened showed the Sons of Thunder once again eager for divine retribution:

> As the time approached for him to be taken up to heaven, Jesus resolutely set out for Jerusalem. And he sent messengers on ahead, who went into a Samaritan village to get things ready for him; but the people there did not welcome him, because he was heading for Jerusalem. When the disciples James and John saw this, they asked, "LORD, do you want us to call fire down from heaven to destroy them?" But Jesus turned and rebuked them. Then he and his disciples went to another village.
> Luke 9:51–55

From James and John's point of view, the Samaritans' insolence was much worse than someone invoking Jesus' name out of imperfect knowledge. They viewed it as willful malice, disobedience to God! They wanted to see fiery destruction consume those Samaritans who had dared to dishonor their Lord. This time, the text implies, Jesus was not so gentle with them, and openly rebuked them for wishing that on people who had acted out of ignorance.

It is interesting to compare this fire-and-brimstone John with the John who appears later in the pages of the New Testament. John never ceased being deeply loyal to Jesus, but he learned to temper that fiery passion with love. He also learned not to act as a self-appointed gatekeeper to the kingdom of God. The first letter of John is a plea for Christian love and forbearance, no matter what, and says that *anyone* who loves has been born of God. What a change!

> Dear friends, let us love one another, for love comes from God. Everyone who loves has been born of God and knows God. Whoever does not love does not know God, because God is love. This is how God showed his love among us: He sent his one and only Son into the world that we might live through him. This is love: not that we loved God, but that he loved us and sent his Son as an atoning sacrifice for our sins. Dear friends, since God so loved us, we also ought to love one another. No one has ever seen God; but if we love one another, God lives in us and his love is made complete in us ... And so we know and rely on the love God has for us. God is love. Whoever lives in love lives in God, and God in them.
>
> 1 John 4:7–12, 16

The community that John was writing to had been torn apart by schism and fighting, by "antichrists" who had denied Jesus and betrayed their church family. But John counseled love and forgiveness, because he had known and loved the incarnate and risen Jesus. That relationship had changed him forever. Jesus' love had transformed John. There's no doubt the change in John was sparked by the friendship and guidance of Jesus Himself. He continually poured into John, and their relationship bore the fruit of that investment.

Of course, that's what God's love does. But that's also what our human friendships should do: encourage each other to be more like Christ. John's journey from an impulsive, judgmental youth to a wise, loving, and welcoming elder of the church shows the power of growing both spiritually and relationally. There are seasoned Christians in my life I reach out to when I'm struggling or trying to make a tough decision. They shoot straight, and they point me right back to God and His truth. There's no rationalizing or feel-good chatter that isn't consistent with God's Word. They aren't afraid to lovingly tell me when I've messed up or gotten off track. It takes maturity to be that kind of friend, and also to receive that kind of advice. It can be easy (and lazy, I'd argue) to tell our friends what they want to hear in the moment. Jesus didn't do that for John, and we shouldn't either.

The Inner Circle

Along with James and Peter, John formed part of the "inner circle" of Jesus' disciples, the ones He took with Him when He was about to reveal a miracle or undergo a great trial. Later, Paul would identify Peter and John as the pillars of the Jerusalem church (Galatians 2:9). John was present with Jesus, as part of this core group, at three crucial events: the raising of Jairus' daughter, the Transfiguration, and the agony in the Garden of Gethsemane. John was there to witness the highest highs and the lowest lows.

When Jesus was approached by Jairus, a synagogue leader, the man was desperate. His daughter was dying. Jesus went with Jairus to his home, and "He did not let anyone follow him except

Peter, James and John the brother of James." (Mark 5:37) Jesus took only these men when He went to raise and restore the young girl. This was the second time that Jesus had revealed Himself as the Lord of the living and the dead. He took His closest friends with him so that they could fully comprehend the truth about Him, but also because He trusted them. In the reality of our lives today, Jesus is also inviting us along to see what He's up to. By being a witness to His grace and power, we grow closer to Him and can know Him more intimately as our Lord and Savior.

Getting to know someone, to fully understand them, takes time. Gradually, Jesus' closest confidants began to discern more about who He was, including Peter.

> **Jesus and his disciples went on to the villages around Caesarea Philippi. On the way he asked them, "Who do people say I am?"**
>
> **They replied, "Some say John the Baptist; others say Elijah; and still others, one of the prophets."**
>
> **"But what about you?" he asked. "Who do you say I am?"**
>
> **Peter answered, "You are the Messiah."**
>
> **Jesus warned them not to tell anyone about him.**
>
> **Mark 8:27–30**

At this point, the disciples had known Jesus for years. Finally, Peter was starting to get it! After this, Jesus began to explicitly reveal to His closest friends the reality of his coming death (Mark 8:31, Luke 9:22).

Six days later, He would reveal even more of His identity. These same three friends saw Jesus in His fully-revealed glory in His Transfiguration, when Jesus appeared in His glorified form talking to Moses and Elijah (Matthew 17:1-8). They were stunned and terrified. Here was their teacher, their friend, and He was suddenly revealed as invested with a power they had clearly never fully realized until that moment. They were so frightened that Peter babbled something about putting up some tents for the heavenly figures.

As He had done before, Jesus instructed them to tell no one what they had seen—at least "until the Son of Man has been raised from the dead." (Matthew 17:9) He wanted their love to overcome their fear, resulting in trusting obedience. And sure enough, "They kept the matter to themselves, discussing what 'rising from the dead' meant." (Mark 9:10) But their fear wasn't completely gone, for the meaning of Jesus' words "was hidden from them, so that they did not grasp it, and they were afraid to ask him about it." (Luke 9:45)

John, Peter, and James were with Jesus in the Garden of Gethsemane. His trust in these three friends was at its greatest there, where they saw not His glory as they had in the Transfiguration, or His power as they had in the raising of Jairus' daughter, but His discouragement and His grief. They witnessed the vulnerability of the Lord of heaven and earth.

> Then Jesus went with his disciples to a place called Gethsemane, and he said to them, "Sit here while I go over there and pray." He took Peter and the two sons of Zebedee along with him, and he began to be sorrowful and troubled. Then he said to them, "My soul is overwhelmed with sorrow to the point of death. Stay here and keep watch with me." Going a little farther, he fell with his face to the ground and prayed, "My Father, if it is possible,

may this cup be taken from me. Yet not as I will, but as you will."

Matthew 26:36-39

Jesus returned to the men He'd asked to pray—not once, not twice, but three times—and found them asleep each time. Their fallible humanity prevented them from being the kind of friends Jesus needed in that moment. *Why,* He must have lamented, *can't they understand what is at stake here*? Why could they not comprehend what their friend was facing? They still didn't understand the gravity of what was to come.

Only John

Let's take a quick flashback to a few days prior to the Garden, in the final week before Jesus' death. You may remember hearing about the bold request James and John's mother made to Christ Himself.

> Then the mother of Zebedee's sons came to Jesus with her sons and, kneeling down, asked a favor of him.
>
> "What is it you want?" he asked.
>
> She said, "Grant that one of these two sons of mine may sit at your right and the other at your left in your kingdom."
>
> "You don't know what you are asking," Jesus said to them. "Can you drink the cup I am going to drink?"
>
> "We can," they answered.

> Jesus said to them, "You will indeed drink from my cup, but to sit at my right or left is not for me to grant. These places belong to those for whom they have been prepared by my Father."
>
> Matthew 20:20–23

We can. These two clearly still had no comprehension of what Jesus would soon suffer. James and John wanted a piece of the action, not realizing that the earthly crown Jesus was destined for would be made of thorns, not gold and precious stones. They were about to learn their idea of the kingdom of God was totally upside down. As that reality began to close in, nearly everyone fled in fear—but not John.

In the final twenty-four hours of Jesus' life, John was there for Him in a way no others were, except for His own mother. When Jesus was arrested, Peter and John followed Him at a safe distance. Only John was "known to the high priest" (John 18:16) and was allowed to follow Jesus into the inner courtyard of the high priest's residence, while Peter had to warm himself at the fire with the servants. This gives John's account an eyewitness quality; it is the testimony of one who was there, and saw the worst of Jesus' trial.

In his account, John kept the focus on Jesus, so we the readers tend to forget that John was describing what he also experienced, all the way through the terrible events that followed. John witnessed the torture, beating, and mocking of Jesus, and His final grueling walk to the site of His execution. John saw all of it, and just as he had witnessed Christ's unspeakable glory at His Transfiguration, John would also see His pain and humiliation. When Jesus was finally nailed to the cross, in the midst of

His agony, He used His remaining strength to give these directions.

> Near the cross of Jesus stood his mother, his mother's sister, Mary the wife of Clopas, and Mary Magdalene. When Jesus saw his mother there, and the disciple whom he loved standing nearby, he said to her, "Woman, here is your son," and to the disciple, "Here is your mother." From that time on, this disciple took her into his home.
>
> John 19:25–27

John was there at the point of Jesus' most excruciating final moments, along with four women. There were no other apostles present. None of them had stayed. They had all scattered—as Jesus had predicted they would—like sheep without a shepherd, cowering in fear.

But not John. The love that had made him follow Jesus through the horror of His last day was with him until the very end. He probably felt the same panic the rest of the disciples did—fear that he would be found guilty by association, fear that he was making himself a target by staying, fear that he would be next. If Jesus' critics decided to round up His disciples, there would be nowhere to hide. They would be fair game. The other disciples made a choice driven by fear, but John was learning something that they did not know, something he would write about years later in his epistle:

> There is no fear in love. But perfect love drives out fear, because fear has to do with punishment. The one who fears is not made perfect in love.
>
> 1 John 4:18.

Finally, True Belief

Just as he had been witness to the events of the crucifixion, John was also an early eyewitness to the Resurrection. Alerted by Mary Magdalene, who was the first to carry the news of the empty tomb to the apostles, Peter and John ran together to see for themselves:

> So Peter and the other disciple started for the tomb. Both were running, but the other disciple outran Peter and reached the tomb first. He bent over and looked in at the strips of linen lying there but did not go in. Then Simon Peter came along behind him and went straight into the tomb. He saw the strips of linen lying there, as well as the cloth that had been wrapped around Jesus' head. The cloth was still lying in its place, separate from the linen. Finally the other disciple, who had reached the tomb first, also went inside. He saw and believed.
>
> John 20:3–8

Before John had received any real confirmation of the Resurrection, he believed in it. All they knew at that point was that Jesus' body wasn't in that tomb. Maybe it had been taken and desecrated. It was unbearable to think that even in His death, the hatred of the Roman and religious authorities would still be raging against Him. Peter and John ran together to the tomb, and the younger John got there first. When John went inside, what he saw was enough for him. If someone had taken His body, why would they have taken off His grave clothes? Why would the head-cloth be folded up separately like that? It didn't make sense, except that it started to, to John.

All that fiery passion that had made John a Son of Thunder apparently lit the flame of belief in his soul. This time, it wasn't Peter putting together the pieces about Jesus' true identity, it was John. His brain made an intuitive leap, powered by the strength of his faith and his love. Without any explanation from anyone, John "believed." He was evangelized, in that moment, not by any words spoken to him, or any sermon preached, or even by any appearance from Jesus Himself. By the time he saw Jesus, John already believed.

Some of us are blessed to have a friend like that, whose faith in us is so overwhelming that they believe we can accomplish incredible things long before we ourselves can see it. It's an amazing feeling to have someone willing to invest that level of confidence in us. *Of course you can do it!* In times and places when no one else believed, John did. And it would sustain him years later as He paid the price for his unwavering belief in his friend, and Savior, Jesus Christ.

John was eventually exiled to the island of Patmos, a remote corner of the Mediterranean. John had been the youngest of the apostles, and he would be the last one to die. They had all been martyred in one way or another. John must have felt left behind—isolated and without his brother apostles and the Church that he had sustained and fed for so long. On Patmos, John's Lord finally appeared to him again—not this time as just the earthly friend and companion that John had known during Jesus' life, but in the fullness of who He was:

On the LORD's Day I was in the Spirit, and I heard behind me a loud voice like a trumpet, which said: "Write on a scroll what you see and send it to the seven churches:

to Ephesus, Smyrna, Pergamum, Thyatira, Sardis, Philadelphia and Laodicea." I turned around to see the voice that was speaking to me. And when I turned, I saw seven golden lampstands, and among the lampstands was someone like a son of man, dressed in a robe reaching down to his feet and with a golden sash around his chest. The hair on his head was white like wool, as white as snow, and his eyes were like blazing fire. His feet were like bronze glowing in a furnace, and his voice was like the sound of rushing waters. In his right hand he held seven stars, and coming out of his mouth was a sharp, double-edged sword. His face was like the sun shining in all its brilliance. When I saw him, I fell at his feet as though dead. Then he placed his right hand on me and said: "Do not be afraid. I am the First and the Last. I am the Living One; I was dead, and now look, I am alive for ever and ever! And I hold the keys of death and Hades."

Revelation 1:10–18

In the visions and revelations that followed, Jesus spoke with the authority of the Alpha and Omega. Incredibly, He took His beloved disciple into heaven itself, and showed him the mysteries that no other eye had ever seen: the angels of the heavenly court, the throne of God, all the miraculous wonder that the human brain could barely fathom. All of this was revealed to John, and entrusted to him to tell to us, his fellow believers, who still read his revelations today.

Revelation is the final word of the New Testament, and scholars have studied it for centuries. It takes dedication, and only heavenly wisdom can help us to fully unlock it. Ultimately, the book is a love story: from Jesus to John in his time of isolation and punishment, from John to us. We are called to share that powerful, beautiful, Christ-driven friendship love until He comes in glory and we can finally say with His beloved John, "Amen! Come, Lord Jesus!"

Prayer: Heavenly Father, You are our truest Friend. Help us to follow Your example of commitment, honesty, and compassion. May we be steadfast in times of testing, and brave in times of trial. Help us to mature in You, to grow in our ability and desire to care for others and to follow Your model of friendship and community. Thank you for displaying the greatest love of all by laying down Your life for ours.

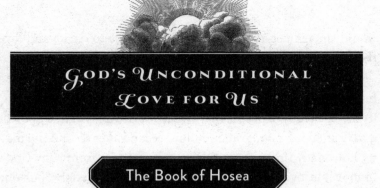

God's Unconditional Love for Us

The Book of Hosea

Nearly every person reading these words has faced heartbreak and betrayal. Few things sting as much as being deceived and double-crossed by someone to whom you entrusted your deepest fears and grandest dreams. It's a shock to the system that bruises every part of your heart and soul, a wound that seems beyond healing—especially in the early days of discovering the wrong that's been done.

Yes, there is risk in love and friendships, but that's no reason to isolate ourselves. In his book *The Four Loves*, C.S. Lewis warned against that very mistake:

> **Love anything, and your heart will certainly be wrung and possibly broken. If you want to make sure of keeping it intact, you must give your heart to no one . . . lock it up safe in the casket or coffin of your selfishness. But in that casket—safe, dark, motionless, airless—it will change. It will not be broken; it will become unbreakable, impenetrable, irredeemable.**[1]

There is no better example of a love willing to take every chance, endure betrayal, and make the ultimate sacrifice than God's unconditional love for you. Even knowing how much we would sin against and reject Him, God chose to create and love the human race.

Imagine having the strength not only to forgive your betrayer, but also to embrace them with love and kindness after their duplicity has been fully exposed. That's what our Heavenly Father does for us day after day, minute after minute, second after second—no matter how many times our faithless hearts wander from Him. God's immovable love for us is a stunning reality portrayed through one of the Old Testament's most difficult stories: Hosea and Gomer.

God's Love Portrayed Through Hosea and Gomer

Hosea was a prophet to the nation of Israel during the time of yet another rebellious detour. There are so many unique things about Hosea, including his marriage—one designed by God Himself. Most of us would think, *Awesome, a match made in heaven!* Not exactly. The marriage we see in the early chapters of the book of Hosea is not one we associate with romance. It's not giddy; it's gritty. But as with every story recorded in the Bible, it's brimming with lessons and truths that apply today as much as they did centuries ago. And it all started with a very difficult assignment for Hosea, directly from God Himself.

> **When the Lord began to speak through Hosea, the Lord said to him, "Go, marry a promiscuous woman and have**

children with her, for like an adulterous wife this land is guilty of unfaithfulness to the LORD."
Hosea 1:2

Whoa. This wasn't a request; it was a command. Was there any hesitation by Hosea? *Lord, it's tough enough to be out here as a prophet to people who really don't want to hear what I have to say. Now you're asking me to choose a less-than-ideal spouse to partner with me in the work?*

At the time of Hosea's ministry, the people of Israel were once again wildly off course. Under King Jeroboam II they were doing well politically and, from a worldly perspective, prospering. Yet their hearts were chasing after everything but the God who had delivered them out of slavery in Egypt hundreds of years earlier. They were also a divided kingdom, with Israel to the north and Judah to the south. Idolatry and immorality were common practices, as were bribery and corruption. God said to Hosea that His people were "guilty of unfaithfulness to the Lord." (Hosea 1:2) Hence, Hosea's heavenly assignment was to enter a marriage that would serve as a real-life picture of the decaying relationship between God and His people.

If Hosea had any hesitation to follow God's direction, we don't see it in Scripture.

So he married Gomer daughter of Diblaim, and she conceived and bore him a son.
Then the LORD said to Hosea, "Call him Jezreel, because I will soon punish the house of Jehu for the massacre at Jezreel, and I will put an end to the kingdom of

Israel. In that day I will break Israel's bow in the Valley of Jezreel."

Hosea 1:3–5

By now you know the importance of names in biblical times, so I need to warn you: buckle up. Jezreel means "scattered" or "God scatters," and that was certainly going to happen to Israel. The Assyrians conquered Israel in 733 BC, and Judah was later overrun by Babylon, literally scattering God's people far and wide.

So who was Jehu and what was the massacre all about? If you track back in time, King Jehu of Israel started the lineage that led to Jeroboam II becoming king. Jehu had killed all the descendants of Ahab in the Valley of Jezreel and established his throne. So it wasn't good news for Jeroboam II that Jehu's house would be snuffed out, and the broader kingdom of Israel would soon be in grave trouble as well.

Hosea and Gomer then had a daughter.

Gomer conceived again and gave birth to a daughter. Then the LORD said to Hosea, "Call her Lo-Ruhamah (which means "not loved"), for I will no longer show love to Israel, that I should at all forgive them."

Hosea 1:6

How would you like to be saddled with the name "not loved"? Some theologians say it can also be interpreted "no mercy." Either way, this tiny baby girl's name bore a devastating prophecy: God had reached a breaking point with the people of Israel. What must people have thought about Hosea's unique marriage? Not only had he married a promiscuous woman, but he was also marking his children with foreboding, depressing names. But God always has a purpose in what He asks of us, and He wasn't done with the truths He was illustrating through Hosea and Gomer yet.

Next came a son.

> After she had weaned Lo-Ruhamah, Gomer had another son. Then the LORD said, "Call him Lo-Ammi (which means "not my people"), for you are not my people, and I am not your God."
> Hosea 1:8–9

How could this be? The Israelites were God's *chosen* people, yet through Hosea's marriage God was telegraphing just how deeply they had damaged their covenant with Him. This proclamation from the Lord feels less like Him distancing Himself from the Israelites and more of a factual statement that *they* were the ones who had walked away from Him.

But even in the grim prognosis modeled in Hosea and Gomer's marriage—and their children's names—God offered hope. Yes, the book of Hosea is filled with warnings and plenty of tough love, but it is also woven through with the unmistakable themes of mercy and restoration. After calling out the breakdown of the Israelites' relationship with Him, God gave a glimpse of the good to come for Israel.

> "Yet the Israelites will be like the sand on the seashore, which cannot be measured or counted. In the place where it was said to them, 'You are not my people,' they will be called 'children of the living God.' The people of Judah and the people of Israel will come together; they will

appoint one leader and will come up out of the land, for
great will be the day of Jezreel."
Hosea 1:10-11

Okay, if you're feeling a bit of whiplash, you're not alone. God
clearly explained how disappointed He was in the people of Israel, calling out their sin and naming names. Then as He so often does for us, He pointed Israel to a future of healing. But they
weren't there yet.

In Hosea 2, the Lord got into the painful details of Israel's
unfaithfulness to Him, once again portrayed in the context of a
crumbling marriage. He said His people should be rebuked and
should "remove the adulterous look from her face." (Hosea 2:2)

> Otherwise I will strip her naked
>   and make her as bare as on the day she was born;
>   I will make her like a desert,
>   turn her into a parched land,
>   and slay her with thirst.
>   I will not show my love to her children,
>   because they are the children of adultery.
>   Their mother has been unfaithful
>   and has conceived them in disgrace.
> Hosea 2:3-5

The people of Israel were openly embracing false gods, chasing
hedonistic pleasures, and losing all spiritual grounding. How it
must have wounded the Lord their God who had delivered them
time and time again, just as it does every time I set my affections
on things other than Him.

The Lord continued by noting that Israel chose to chase "lovers," crediting them for the good things in life (Hosea 2:5), blinded—whether willfully or not—to the fact that those gifts were from God. Not only that, but Israel also took those blessings *from* the Lord and offered them *to* a false god.

> She has not acknowledged that I was the one
> who gave her the grain, the new wine and oil,
> who lavished on her the silver and gold—
> which they used for Baal.
> Hosea 2:8

Despite the people's straying, I love what Hosea's story also shows us about God's heart—He would not give up His people without a fight.

> Therefore I will block her path with thornbushes;
> I will wall her in so that she cannot find her way.
> She will chase after her lovers but not catch them;
> she will look for them but not find them.
> Then she will say,
> "I will go back to my husband as at first,
> for then I was better off than now."
> Hosea 2:6–7

God explained that He would make life difficult for Israel, so that His people would find their way back to Him. I'm reminded of the decades the Israelites spent wandering in the wilderness because of their own stubbornness.

God often allows us to have a season in a spiritual desert, not because He doesn't love us—but precisely because He *does*. We can waste plenty of time chasing things of this world that—at best—offer only temporary peace or satisfaction. But we will come to the end of our ropes when we realize that nothing short of God Himself will ever satisfy our deepest longings, and the more we run from His unconditional love for us, the more we prolong our time of brokenness and separation from our Heavenly Father.

Hosea 2:9-13 outlined just how tough things would get before God would reunite with His people. God vowed to take back His gifts (v. 9), "expose [Israel's] lewdness," (v. 10) stop all her celebrations (v. 11), ruin the vines and fig trees she claimed were "pay from her lovers," (v. 12) and punish her for worshipping the false god Baal and forgetting about Him (v. 13).

Yet amid all that pain, once He had Israel's attention, God vowed to win her back.

> Therefore I am now going to allure her;
> > I will lead her into the wilderness
> > and speak tenderly to her.
> Hosea 2:14

Harsh words, fueled by God's wrath at His people's adulterous rejection, would be replaced with renewal and redemption. The Lord promised to "give back [Israel's] vineyards," (v. 15) to once again be referred to as Israel's "husband" rather than "master," (v. 15) and to wipe out battles and danger "so that all may lie down in safety." (v. 18) The relationship would be restored.

> I will betroth you to me forever;
> > I will betroth you in righteousness and justice,

in love and compassion.
I will betroth you in faithfulness,
and you will acknowledge the LORD.
Hosea 2:19–20

The word translated as "love" in verse 19 is a Hebrew word that experts say is difficult to truly translate: *hesed*. One Old Testament dictionary described it this way:

> A covenant term, wrapping up in itself all the positive attributes of God: love, covenant faithfulness, mercy, grace, kindness, loyalty—in short acts of devotion and loving-kindness that go beyond the requirements of duty.[2]

God wasn't simply telling the people of Israel they could come home to Him; He was pledging something much more encompassing: an active embrace of commitment and compassion.

Things would only get better from there! God vowed to bring blessings on the land and to finally undo those demoralizing names he'd assigned to Hosea's offspring.

I will plant her for myself in the land;
  I will show my love to the one I called "Not my loved one."
  I will say to those called "Not my people," "You are my people";
  and they will say, "You are my God."
Hosea 2:23

These words of expectation about the restoration to come between God and His people would be lived out in the marriage of

Hosea and Gomer for all the people to see. So, now for the rest of his story.

We return to the prophet's broken home in Hosea 3.

The LORD said to me, "Go, show your love to your wife again, though she is loved by another man and is an adulteress. Love her as the LORD loves the Israelites, though they turn to other gods ..."

Hosea 3:1

While still married to Hosea, Gomer had run into the arms of another man, returning to her promiscuous ways. God knew this would happen, but I wonder if Hosea did too. He married a woman who was openly flaunting her sexual sin, but had Hosea hoped his love and attention would change his wife's heart from that point forward? While Gomer was unfaithful to her husband—as the people of Israel were unfaithful to the Lord, Hosea made the difficult choice to abide in God's plan. The text does not tell us that Gomer had abandoned her adulterous ways at this point. Hosea wasn't instructed to wait until she got her act together. Instead, God told Hosea to go redeem his wife while she was still living in sin. Sound familiar? More on that to come.

As a picture of how God redeemed Israel, and as He does for us, Hosea went and bought his wife back. Whether it was out of prostitution or some other type of slavery, Gomer's husband redeemed her, paying the price to buy her freedom. But God didn't tell Hosea just to carry out a transaction and bring her home. No, He specifically told Hosea to "show your love to your wife." (Hosea 3:1) The prophet took Gomer home and told her to be faithful, pledging that he would do the same for her.

Here's the thing—we all want to be Hosea in this story, but we're Gomer. We desire to be the hero, but on a spiritual level we're always going to be the one who needs to be rescued. It's easy to point the finger elsewhere, but what we usually need is a mirror. God's boundless love for us is limitless, meaning He is always pursuing us and calling for us to abandon our selfish wanderings. Think of all the beautiful stories stitched through the Old Testament in a tapestry of forgiveness and mercy every time Israel rejected God's principles and plans, fell into tragic circumstances, begged for His redemption and saw it delivered.

God repeatedly uses the metaphor of marriage to help us understand His devotion to us and our relationship past, present, and future. Here in Isaiah:

"For your Maker is your husband—
  the LORD Almighty is his name—
  the Holy One of Israel is your Redeemer;
  he is called the God of all the earth.
  The LORD will call you back
  as if you were a wife deserted and distressed in spirit—
  a wife who married young,
  only to be rejected," says your God.
  "For a brief moment I abandoned you,
  but with deep compassion I will bring you back.
  In a surge of anger
  I hid my face from you for a moment,
  but with everlasting kindness
  I will have compassion on you,"
  says the LORD your Redeemer.
  Isaiah 54:5-8

Later in Isaiah 62:5 He declares, "As a bridegroom rejoices over a bride, so your God will rejoice over you."

God's Love Displayed Through Jesus Christ

In the New Testament, Jesus often painted the same picture of God's unconditional love for us using the picture of a marriage relationship. In Matthew 9, He referred to Himself as "the bridegroom." Ephesians 5 is rich with the imagery of Christ as Redeemer and Husband, while the church is His beloved bride. In telling earthly husbands they should love their wives "as their own bodies," the apostle Paul adds, "I am actually speaking with reference to Christ and the church." (Ephesians 5:28, 32)

I'm deeply moved by the New Testament's many reminders about Christ's agape love for us, so beautifully stated by Paul in Romans 5:

> Very rarely will anyone die for a righteous person, though for a good person someone might possibly dare to die. But God demonstrates his own love for us in this: While we were still sinners, Christ died for us.
> Romans 5:7–8

Think about the person you love most in this world. Would you jump in front of a train to push your loved one to safety? Many of us would say, "Yes, their life is worth it." Now close your eyes and get a clear mental image of the person who has hurt you more than anyone else. It could even be a hated historical figure who wreaked havoc on the world and was responsible for brutal torture and countless deaths. What about that person? Would you lift even a single finger to make sure they escaped harm? That's exactly what Jesus did . . . willingly.

The fact is, Jesus knew we could never save ourselves. He knew we would lie, cheat, steal, and much worse. But He never said, *I'm willing to be beaten and crucified for people who fibbed on their tax returns, but not for a murderer.* That's because even one sin separates us from God, breaks our ability to commune with Him, and leaves us desperately alone. It's often easy for us to look around this fallen world and feel pretty good about how our sins stack up against someone else's. Gossip? Eh, it's not as bad as bank robbery. White lies? They're harmless compared to bombing innocent civilians. Guess what, they all have the same spiritual impact—eternal separation from God. That's why it's so incredibly dangerous to take even one step up onto that pedestal where we want to imagine we live.

On the cross, Jesus Christ took upon himself every ugly sin that's ever been—and ever will be—committed. He knew just how deeply we would need a Savior, and with His unmatched, unlimited love for us, He decided to step into the abyss and bear our sin for us. I often have a difficult time putting my head around that level of compassion and sacrifice. The Bible makes it clear the choice was not an easy one for the Son of God. Simple? Necessary? Yes and yes. Difficult? Also yes.

As Christ prayed in the garden of Gethsemane before He was taken into custody and crucified, Luke 22:44 tells us:

And being in anguish, he prayed more earnestly, and his sweat was like drops of blood falling to the ground.

Matthew 26:38–39 records His struggle this way:

> Then [Jesus] said to them, "My soul is overwhelmed with sorrow to the point of death. Stay here and keep watch with me."
>
> Going a little further, he fell with his face to the ground and prayed, "My Father, if it is possible, may this cup be taken from me. Yet not as I will, but as you will."

Mark 14 repeats Christ's statement that his soul was overwhelmed with sorrow "to the point of death." (Mark 14:34)

As fully God, Jesus knew exactly what He was going to suffer. He had total awareness of the physical beating, torture, and excruciating death that was to come. And He also was fully aware of the many betrayals He would face by people who had proclaimed Him as Messiah. He knew His own Father would turn His back on Him for a time. It is painful and crushing to attempt to put ourselves in that place mentally. How could you process the knowledge that you would be tormented physically and emotionally beyond the limits of what you could bear and still choose to walk forward? Not just for your beloved child or spouse or friend, but for the worst human being ever to walk this earth? Who among us would agree to do it?

Christ's choice to willingly walk to His own crucifixion was motivated by His unconditional love for us. Sit with that for a minute. The Creator of this universe lowered Himself to become human and experience every temptation and trial we face, knowing His life on earth would ultimately end with someone close to Him delivering Him into the very hands that would brutally torture and execute Him. Before you ever existed, God loved you that much.

Psalm 139:16 tells us, "All the days ordained for me were written in [God's] book before one of them came to be." Jesus chose to go to the cross for you knowing everything about your life, every good and bad choice you would make, every regret you would ever have, and all the times you would choose something—or someone—other than Him.

> But because of his great love for us, God, who is rich in mercy, made us alive with Christ even when we were dead in transgressions—it is by grace you have been saved.
> Ephesians 2:4-5

Love. Grace. Mercy. These aren't just things God gives us. They are who He is. First John 4:8 states simply: "God is love." That chapter goes on to remind us this isn't a conditional deal.

> This is love: not that we loved God, but that he loved us and sent his Son as an atoning sacrifice for our sins.
> 1 John 4:10

We don't have to show up and make our case in order to get God's attention or affection. We could never convince a judge or jury we are worthy of God's love, and thank goodness we don't have to! No, 1 John 4 makes it clear that God's love flows to us without reservation or bargaining.

We should be overjoyed at the knowledge of God's unconditional, no-need-to-earn-it love for us. What enormous comfort and glorious reassurance that He isn't going anywhere. But we can't leave it there. By showering us with His agape love, our Savior also cultivates our ability to share it with others, and He expects us to. We show our love to the Father by loving the way He does. In Matthew 5, Jesus instructed His disciples:

> But I tell you, love your enemies and pray for those who persecute you, that you may be children of your Father in heaven.
> Matthew 5:44–45

Jesus told us to model the gracious gift we've been given. We must exercise a love that goes beyond earthly, human boundaries. Sure it's easy to love the people who already love us, but Christ cautioned, "Are not even the tax collectors doing that?" (Matthew 5:46) He instead urged us to love others—including those who hurt us—with the same perfect love our Heavenly Father extends to us.

Philippians 2 commands us to value others and their interests above our own. Romans 15:2 urges us to build up our neighbors. First Corinthians 10:24 couldn't make it any clearer: "No one should seek their own good, but the good of others." Remember in 1 John 4:8 where we were told God Himself is love? Just three verses later, the apostle John admonished believers to love one another in the way God loves us (1 John 4:11).

These teachings go against nearly everything the world tells us to do. In today's society, we're urged to do what makes us feel good and not worry about the impact on anyone else. Recent headlines, blogs, and book titles blare things like: "5 Ways to Make Yourself Happier," "Why You Should Try to Be More Selfish," "Key to Happiness: How to Put Yourself First," and the list goes on. What a contrast to the selfless, loving actions of Jesus! In addition to His decision to sacrifice heavenly comfort so that He could come and die for every single human who will ever exist, He was also in the trenches going to people in desperate need—specifically people who could never repay Him. That's the very definition of agape. God knew we could never give Him anything of value in return for His love, so He covers us in a love that is totally unmerited and has zero strings attached.

In John 8, Jesus went to a woman who had been caught in adultery and was about to be stoned to death. We watch as He shamed her accusers and covered her in forgiveness. In Mark 5 and Luke 8 we witness His approval wash over a woman who was essentially an outcast with no hope because of a long-term illness that rendered her "unclean" in most people's eyes. Luke 19 reveals the story of Jesus going straight to one of the most hated men in his community, Zacchaeus the tax collector. As Christ asked to spend time with the man, the Bible tells us people muttered about Him going to be "the guest of a sinner." (v. 7) Well, goodness, if Jesus couldn't hang with sinners, there would be no one for Him to fellowship with at all!

There is great beauty in the story of Jesus' interaction with the Samaritan woman at the well in John 4. Not only did the Samaritans and Jews have deep divisions and hostility toward one another, but this particular woman was also living on the very fringes of her community after a long string of failed marriages and relationships. Rather than shame or ignore her, Christ shared a message of salvation and hope with her. He offered her the "living water" of salvation, and revealed He was the Messiah she was awaiting.

> Just then his disciples returned and were surprised to find him talking with a woman. But no one asked, "What do you want?" or "Why are you talking with her?"
> John 4:27

Don't you love that? The disciples knew that norms and traditions of the day would not have encouraged, or even permitted, this interaction between Jesus and a Samaritan woman. But because of the up-close-and-personal way they had seen Jesus live, going to the "least of these," (Matthew 25:40) they didn't even bother to question what He was doing. Christ had modeled genuine compassion time and again in their presence.

We're repeatedly admonished in Scripture that we can't leave that work to Jesus alone. Recall His words in Matthew 25, identifying the ones who will be a part of His ultimate kingdom.

> "'For I was hungry and you gave me something to eat, I was thirsty and you gave me something to drink, I was a stranger and you invited me in, I needed clothes and you clothed me, I was sick and you looked after me, I was in prison and you came to visit me.'
>
> "Then the righteous will answer him, 'Lord, when did we see you hungry and feed you, or thirsty and give you something to drink? When did we see you a stranger and invite you in, or needing clothes and clothe you? When did we see you sick or in prison and go to visit you?'

"The King will reply, 'Truly I tell you, whatever you did for one of the least of these brothers and sisters of mine, you did for me.'"
  Matthew 25:35–40

When He was asked by a religious teacher of the day what was the most important commandment, Jesus was clear:

"Love the LORD your God with all your heart and with all your soul and with all your mind and with all your strength." The second is this: "Love your neighbor as yourself." There is no commandment greater than these.
  Mark 12:30–31

He didn't separate the directive that we love God from the mandate that we also love our neighbors as much as we love ourselves. (And let's be honest, we're born selfish!) No one models obedience to these commands better than my mom. I've written and talked about her selflessness many times. She doesn't avoid people who are in trouble, in messy situations, or completely unable to ever return any of her service or gifts. She *runs* to those people. That's agape love.

So, where is there more room for this in my life? In your life? Who are we to hoard the glorious legacy of God's unlimited, unconditional, redemptive, merciful love? The Bible is filled with human variations of this precious gift, our best attempts at the unconditional love only God can provide in its purest form. The Lord knows we will often fail in our attempts, but He calls us to try. What a sad dead end it would be for us simply to absorb God's all-encompassing agape love for ourselves and not share it with a world so desperately in need of it. Take joy in His adoration of you, and go make sure others know the good news!

> For I am convinced that neither death nor life, neither angels nor demons, neither the present nor the future, nor any powers, neither height nor depth, nor anything else in all creation, will be able to separate us from the love of God that is in Christ Jesus our LORD.
> Romans 8:28–29

Prayer: Heavenly Father, thank you for the precious gift of Your unending love. Help me to remember that nothing I have done or ever will do could begin to outweigh Your unlimited mercy and grace. Long before I existed, You knew all of my days, and loved me unconditionally and without reservation. May I rest in that immovable truth! Expand my heart to share Your love with others, selflessly and with great joy.

ACKNOWLEDGMENTS

It is an incredible blessing to share the beautiful, inspiring truths of God's Word in this book, and none of it happens by chance. I'm grateful to every single Sunday School teacher who volunteered their time and invested in my fidgety little soul each week at church. And to all those dedicated folks who staffed the A.W.A.N.A program on Wednesday nights to show me how to memorize the Bible verses I can still quote today: Thank you. Kindergarten through twelfth grade I was blessed with teachers each year who cared even more about my spiritual growth than my quarterly report cards. And there aren't words that can adequately capture how deeply grateful I am for every professor, adviser, and resident assistant at Liberty University who stood in the gap when I struggled to make my faith truly personal. God bless you.

All of those people built the foundation for the words you find in these pages. They planted seeds many of them never actually got to see bear fruit. They invested in the next generation, and I pray this book will be credited to their legacies.

The power of my praying Momma, Marie, is unmatched. Her endless encouragement and cheerleading, guided by her unshakable faith, continue to sustain and challenge me on every adventure. Mary Grace Dupree, your insights and ideas are priceless. Jennifer Stair, your wisdom and heart for these stories is unmatched. Hannah Long, what a treasure you are! It's nearly unbelievable to me how each of these women came together in order to make this book possible, but the truth is: God connected us and He works through each of us to create something infinitely better than the sum of our parts.

Lisa Sharkey, you are tireless in making sure the world knows how to find these stories of God's goodness. Jason Klarman, thank you for launching these gems into the universe and understanding how much people would be blessed by them. Michael Tammero, you believed from the beginning! Look at what you guys have accomplished!

Olivia, your expertise and tenacity made this opportunity a reality. Tessa, you are a calendar-whisperer. From podcasts to planes, trains, and automobiles you keep me in check. I'll always have a Diet Coke in the fridge for you. Heartfelt thanks to Irena Briganti and our incredible media relations team at Fox, especially Alexandria Coscia and Caley Cronin for their tireless efforts 365 days a year.

Writing each of the chapters about friendships reminded me how deeply blessed I am by the Lord's goodness in the form of the amazing, unconventional women I get to do life with. Through every season, every high and low, I have somewhere to turn. The Coraggios and The Sorority are made up of my female friends who understand the cone of silence and who show up when life gets dicey. They make me laugh, and they've held me when I've cried. They've been the earthly vessels for Christ's love and truth.

But nothing meaningful in my world would get done without the love of my life, Sheldon. Shel—you are unflinchingly strong—especially in the places where I'm most weak. You know how to bind up my heart when it's been wounded, and how to reassure me that "everything is going to be ok." All of my best adventures are with you! You make order out of chaos. You are my fiercest protector. God blessed me with all the best things in the pages of this book—romance and true friendship—when He gave me you. You are my very best friend, and you're also smoking hot.

To my Heavenly Father be all glory. Thank You for ransoming my soul, and for reminding me with every passing year that nothing can ever separate me from Your all-consuming love. May everyone who reads these pages know that truth to the deepest parts of their hearts.

NOTES

SONG OF SOLOMON: THE GIFT OF LOVE

1. Origen translated by R.P. Lawson, *The Song of Songs Commentary and Homilies* (New York: Newman Press, 1956), 23.

ADAM AND EVE: THE ORIGINAL LOVE STORY

1. Matthew Henry, "Commentary on the Whole Bible: Genesis 2:21–25," accessed via Bible Gateway, November 27, 2022.

GOD'S UNCONDITIONAL LOVE FOR US

1. C.S. Lewis, *The Four Loves* (New York: Harcourt, 1971), 121.
2. Tremper Longman III and Peter Enns, eds., *Dictionary of the Old Testament: Wisdom, Poetry and Writings* (InterVarsity Press: Downers Grove, IL, 2020), 6.1.3.

Shannon Bream is the author of the number one *New York Times* bestsellers *The Women of the Bible Speak* and *The Mothers and Daughters of the Bible Speak,* the anchor of *Fox News Sunday,* and the Fox News Channel's chief legal correspondent. She has covered landmark cases at the Supreme Court and heated political campaigns and policy battles from the White House to Capitol Hill.